WRITE IT RIGHT

Beginning Handwriting and Composition for Sudents of ESL

Helen Abdulaziz
Ellen Shenkarow

Center for English as a Second Language
University of Arizona

PRENTICE-HALL
Englewood Cliffs, New Jersey 07632

Editorial/production supervision and
interior design: Lori L. Baronian
Cover design: Lundgren Graphics, Ltd.
Manufacturing buyer: Harry Baisley

Printed in the United States of America
10 9 8 7 6 5 4 3 2 1

ISBN 0-13-969437-4   01

Prentice-Hall International (UK) Limited, *London*
Prentice-Hall of Australia Pty. Limited, *Sydney*
Prentice-Hall Canada Inc., *Toronto*
Prentice-Hall Hispanoamericana, S.A., *Mexico*
Prentice-Hall of India Private Limited, *New Delhi*
Prentice-Hall of Japan, Inc., *Tokyo*
Prentice-Hall of Southeast Asia Pte. Ltd., *Singapore*
Editora Prentice-Hall do Brasil, Ltda., *Rio de Janeiro*
Whitehall Books Limited, *Wellington, New Zealand*

To our families,
Mohyeddin, Hana, Mona,
Mark, Maria, Lucy

CONTENTS

PREFACE

Write it Right is a composition text for ESL students with no previous knowledge of English. Beginning with the alphabet and an easy-to-master form of handwriting, it progresses to writing vocabulary, simple sentence patterns, and to the production of simple paragraphs. The text guides the ESL student with controlled writing exercises. The text teaches writing specifically, and is designed so that writing classes will no longer have to rely on texts written for spoken or reading classes. In contrast to the typical beginning ESL text, *Write It Right* contains easy-to-grasp explanations of key grammatical concepts. An effort is made to include a wide variety of interesting composition topics ranging from buying a car to camping. Although it is designed primarily for 0-level students who are literate in their own languages, the first ten lessons can be used with students who are illiterate in their own languages. These students progress more slowly than students who are already literate in one language.

Many adult students whose native alphabet is not Roman have great difficulty with penmanship, which frustrates both students and teachers. Therefore, this text teaches a form of script handwriting that is neither block printing nor cursive, but is an acceptable form of script that enables students to write English legibly. Because it has been noted that many native writers do not use cursive script, students are not required to write it.

The text consists of three parts. The major goal of the first part (Unit I) is legible handwriting. It begins with the alphabet written in script and includes copying exercises that aid not only in developing legible penmanship, but also in learning basic vocabulary. Because we assume that students have had very little or no previous experience writing English, we believe that before they can do much original writing, they need to master the orthography, penmanship, and a few basic structures of English. Students who are already literate in the Roman alphabet and have legible penmanship may complete Lesson 1 in much less time than those who are learning the Roman alphabet for the first time. Lessons 2–10 continue to provide practice in script, using fundamental English sentences and structures such as the verb *to be* in the present and past, singular and plural nouns and pronouns, adjectives, and possessives. Vocabulary and ideas are introduced in pictures, making translation from the student's native language rarely necessary. Grammatical structures required in the writing exercises are introduced and reviewed systematically. Not all English structures are taught, as it is expected that students will be using other texts and learning from other sources. Ours is primarily a writing text, not a comprehensive grammar.

In order to motivate students to write freely and to accommodate varying writing abilities in a class, we have provided as many opportunities as possible for students to write original pieces on topics related to their own experiences. We also encourage students to keep journals as soon as possible. Journals provide students with the opportunity to write as much as they can on topics of their choice while serving as a source of ideas for more formal compositions later.

Lessons 11–20 introduce sentence patterns using present, past, future, and continuous, the modals, adverb clauses of time and result, and more vocabulary. The major objective of these lessons is mastery of simple sentences and joining sentences. Patterns are introduced in content units with exercises emphasizing composition skills rather than spoken or reading skills. Students are asked to write simple sentences and later to coordinate and subordinate ideas. Vocabulary is carefully controlled; it is either introduced in pictures or was previously encountered in the first ten lessons. An attempt is made to "recycle" content areas so the words introduced earlier will be reused both in these lessons and later in simple paragraphs.

Lessons 21–24 introduce no new grammatical structures; they concentrate on the use of transitions, coordination, subordination, and more specifically, on composition. New content words are still introduced by pictures; however, more reliance is placed on gaining meaning from written examples. Here, having been given the vocabulary and main idea, students are asked to start writing paragraphs using organizational patterns including instruction, description, chronology, comparison, and contrast. Revising and editing will be emphasized in this section, as students are encouraged to rewrite and revise their compositions.

Upon completion of this text, the student will have mastered the following writing skills: legible penmanship; vocabulary acquisition, including spelling, recognition, and production of simple sentences; recognition and production of simple paragraphs using organizational patterns that include instruction, description, chronology, comparison, and contrast.

Lesson Format

Each lesson contains a variety of exercises that are useful for practicing sentence structures, vocabulary, punctuation, and paragraph development.

Grammar

The authors believe that at this level grammar is taught more by example than by explanation. Therefore, the discussions of grammar boxed in this text give examples and very brief statements about the grammatical point. It is expected that individual teachers will give more detailed explanations in class as necessary and depending on the level of the class. The grammatical explanations in the text are intended mainly as a reference and reminder for the student.

Beginning with Lesson 11, introductory sentences at the beginning of the lesson bring in new vocabulary and grammatical patterns in context, often accompanied by a picture. These sentences display patterns and sentences to be manipulated later in the lesson.

There are three types of exercise in each lesson. The first is the simple, fill-in-the-blank type. Its purpose is to allow the student to practice recognition of the target structures. Such an exercise may require only copying or manipulation to produce the desired structures. The second exercise requires the production of partial sentences or sentence combining. Such an exercise sometimes repeats the previous one. It is hoped that their repetitiveness will increase fluency and confidence for the true beginner. More advanced students will not find it necessary to do all these exercises, and may skip directly to the third set of exercises—the writing practice.

Writing Practice Exercises

Writing Practice exercises require the production of several sentences on a related topic, and they can be used for paragraph development. Here again the teacher will follow different paths depending on the level and abilities of the class. Students are first asked to write a series of sentences on a topic. The teacher can correct these sentences grammatically, supply needed vocabulary and suggest additional ideas. At the same time, the teacher should control the organization of the developing paragraph without necessarily trying to explain it to the student. After this discussion with the teacher, the student is asked to revise and rewrite in paragraph form.

Punctuation

Punctuation practice is included wherever a new punctuation point occurs. The new punctuation is explained, and followed by a practice exercise.

Dictation

In Lessons 1–10, the purpose of the dictation is to enable the student to review the structures, learn vocabulary, and memorize spelling. Lessons 11–20 have two additional purposes: to familiarize the student with paragraph form and to allow them to express their own ideas. At this level, the teacher, however, must guide paragraph organization and make sure that the length of the dictation corresponds to the ability of the class. We suggest the following dictation procedure:

1. class discussion of topic
2. write several ideas on board
3. someone, probably the teacher, supplies the main idea sentence
4. write the paragraph on the board
5. students copy the paragraph in their book
6. teacher should check the copied dictation for accuracy
7. practice for homework
8. teacher later dictates a similar paragraph in class

Steps 2–6 may not be necessary for a more advanced class. After going over the introductory sentences on the first pages of the lesson, the teacher may simply tell the students to prepare for a dictation the next day. The teacher can write a simple paragraph based on the content and using the new structures.

The following are two sample dictations that were generated by a beginning composition class.

George wants to buy a car. He needs a big car because he has three children. He needs to buy a used car because he doesn't have enough money. He needs to borrow $2000. (Lesson 11)

The Olympic games began in Greece. Hercules was the best athlete. Now, athletes compete in individual and team events. They each want to win a gold medal for their country. The games are internationally important. (Lesson 15)

Unit I
Lesson 1

THE ALPHABET

Teacher instructions

1. Explain the concept of margins on paper.

2. Demonstrate the concept of reading from left to right. Have students open a text-book and follow along with you as you look at or read the words from left to right. It's important to emphasize this concept from the beginning for students whose native alphabet is written from right to left.

3. Demonstrate the concept of writing from left to right. Look at the short paragraph in Figure 1–1 as an example. Write a few sentences on the blackboard as further illustration.

4. ↑∩ Arrows will be used as guides in letter formation. They indicate the direction the pencil should go.

    ᵃ→A A small number 2 indicates that a second stroke is necessary.

    ↓↑B Two arrows in opposite directions indicate retracing. Do not raise the pencil.

5. Emphasize the importance of good posture when writing. It will minimize backache. (See Figure 1–2.)

6. When students have proceeded to write words in Lesson 1, point out how letter spacing in one word is different from spacing between two words. Many students have a tendency to run together two or three words, so that they have the appearance of one word. Students need to be careful of spacing between words.

Objectives of lessons 1–10 in order of importance:

> penmanship
>
> recognition of typed and written letters
>
> vocabulary acquisition (after lesson 1)
>
> spelling of new vocabulary
>
> basic structural patterns

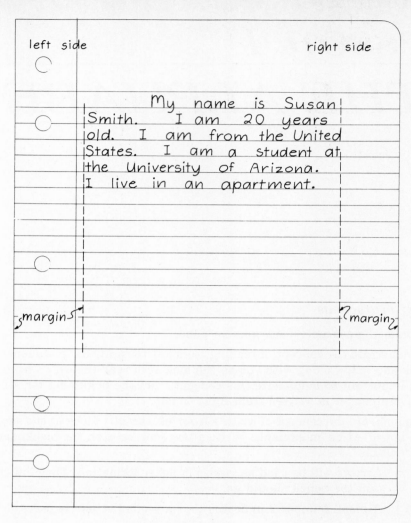

left side   right side

> My name is Susan Smith. I am 20 years old. I am from the United States. I am a student at the University of Arizona. I live in an apartment.

margin   margin

FIGURE 1–1

FIGURE 1–2

Look at the handwritten letters. Read them. Read across the page from left to right. Learn the names of the letters.

Aa Bb Cc Dd Ee Ff Gg

Hh Ii Jj Kk Ll Mm Nn

Oo Pp Qq Rr Ss Tt Uu

Vv Ww Xx Yy Zz

Look at the typed letters. Read them. Read across the page from left to right. Practice the names of the letters.

A a	B b	C c	D d	E e	F f	G g
H h	I i	J j	K k	L l	M m	N n
O o	P p	Q q	R r	S s	T t	U u
V v	W w	X x	Y y	Z z		

Read the letters. Read across each group from left to right. Learn the names of the letters.

1. A E I O U	7. B P V D T R	13. C S Z X
2. a c e i o	8. b d f h k l	14. _fghjk_
3. _C S Z_	9. F V K G J H	15. m n r u v w
4. l i j k e	10. M N W V B P	16. _l i k l_
5. _M N W_	11. s x z c e	17. a e i o u
6. W Y X S Z	12. _m n r u v_	18. _Q P R A_

A E I O U are vowels. All the other letters are consonants.

Big letters are capital letters. A A   B B   c C   D D
Small letters are lowercase letters. a a   b b   c c   d d

Read the letters. Then write each letter several times. Write across the page from left to right.

A _A A A_

a _a a a_

B _B B B_

b _b b b_

c C̄ C C _____

c c̄ c c _____

D D D D _____

d d d d _____

EXERCISE A

Read the letters. Circle the letters *a* and *d*, both capital and lowercase. First look at the examples.

(A)(d) b c C d b A a B c D b d A c a _____

EXERCISE B

Read the letters. Circle the letter that is the same as the first letter. Look at the example.

1. a   c (a) b d
2. d   b d c a
3. b   d c b a
4. c   a b d c
5. d   c d b a

6. C   A D C B
7. A   D C A B
8. B   A B A C
9. D   D C C A
10. B   A A B D

EXERCISE C

Read the letter. Write it after looking at the example.

B B   c ___   D ___   A ___   a ___   b ___   d ___   C ___

EXERCISE D

Look at the picture. Read the word, then copy each word two times. Say the word and listen to the sounds.

dab   add   dad   cab

EXERCISE E

Read the words. Put them in the order of the alphabet. This is called alphabetical order. When the first letter is the same, look at the next letter. First look at the example.

1. dad   cab   add   <u>add cab dad</u>

2. add   dab   cab   _____

3. dad   dab   add   _____

Read the letters. Then write each letter several times. Write across the page from left to right.

E   E E E _____

e   e e e _____

F   F F F _____

f   f f f _____

G   G G G _____

g   g g g _____

H   H H H _____

h   h h h _____

EXERCISE A

Read the letters. Circle the capital and lowercase letters *e* and *h,* as in the examples.

E h g G F f e h E g e h H E

F f e g G h H f h G g G e

EXERCISE B

Read the letters. Circle the one that is the same as the first letter, as in the example.

1. F   HFCA   6. e   acea

2. H   FEHG   7. g   hgfe

3. G   HFGB   8. h   fhbd

4. A   CBEA   9. f   bhfd

5. E   EFCB   10. b   dbch

EXERCISE C

Read the letters. Copy them after looking at the example.

e _e_ E ___ f ___ H ___ G ___ g ___ e ___ F ___

g ___ h ___ H ___ F ___ f ___ e ___ E ___ H ___

EXERCISE D

Read the letters. Now listen to the teacher. The teacher will read one letter from each group. Circle it.

1. a e c   6. H G B
2. d b e   7. D E C
3. f g b   8. F H D
4. d b f   9. G A C
5. e c a   10. B F D

EXERCISE E

Look at the pictures. Read the words, then write each word two times. Say the words and listen to the sounds.

bag   hag   flag

beef   feed

bead   beach   leaf

6

EXERCISE F

Read the words. Put them in alphabetical order, as in the example. When the first letter is the same, look at the next letter.

1. bead   feed   leaf   bead   feed   leaf
2. flag   hag   bag   _____
3. beach   dab   hag   _____
4. cab   beef   add   _____
5. dad   flag   beach   _____
6. beef   bead   feed   _____

Dictation. Study these letters and words. Your teacher will dictate some of them.

1. Write these letters.

   b d f h g a c e _____

2. Write these words.

   add   add   cab   _____
   flag   _____   beef   _____
   leaf   _____   bead   _____

Read the letters. Then write each letter several times. Write across the page from left to right.

I   I I I _____
i   i i i _____
J   J J J _____
j   j j j _____
K   K K k _____
k   K k k _____
L   L L L _____
l   l l l _____

EXERCISE A

Read the letters. Now listen to the teacher. The teacher will read two letters from each group. Circle them.

1. fe ka ga   4. da ba da
2. Bi Ci Di   5. fe ke ka
3. je ge ke   6. li Ia Le

EXERCISE B

Look at the pictures. Read the words, then write them. Say the words and listen to the sounds.

hill   fall   bell

kick   jack   deck

kid   gab   bed

EXERCISE C

Read the words. Write them in alphabetical order after looking at the example.

1. cab	bell	add	add bell cab
2. gab	hill	feed	_____
3. deck	fall	bell	_____
4. kid	gab	bed	_____
5. bell	hill	fall	_____

EXERCISE D

Put these groups of letters in alphabetical order, as in the example. When the first letter is the same, look at the next letter.

1.	be	bi	ba	ba be bi
2.	cl	ce	ci	_____
3.	fe	fl	fa	_____
4.	ba	be	bi	_____

8

5.   hei   hea   hie   _____

6.   jac   jai   jal   _____

Read the letters. Then write each letter several times. Write across the page from left to right.

M $^1\downarrow$m m _____

m $^1\downarrow$m m _____

N $\downarrow$N N _____

n $\downarrow$n n _____

O O O _____

o o o _____

P P P _____

p P P _____

EXERCISE A

Read the letters. Now listen to the teacher. The teacher will read two letters from each group. Circle them.

1. oa na ma   4. pa ba da

2. me ke ne   5. mo po no

3. pi ci be   6. oa ai oo

EXERCISE B

Read the letters. Circle the ones that are the same as the first letters, as in the example.

1. pe (pe) pi pl   5. be bi be ba

2. oa ao oa oo   6. mi me mn mi

3. oo ao oo oa   7. ll le kl ll

4. ga ja ga pa   8. kl kl lk ll

EXERCISE C

Read the letters. Write them. First look at the example.

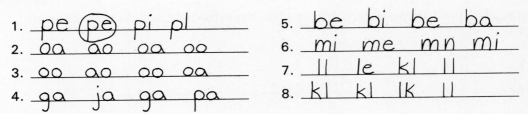

Ab Ab   Ba ____   Jo ____   Ga ____   Ce ____   Mo ____   Pa ____

ni ____   op ____   pi ____   na ____   pe ____   no ____   ob ____

EXERCISE D

Look at the pictures. Read the words, then copy them once. Say the words and listen to the sounds.

mop	cap	pin	pan
mope	cape	pine	pane
mend	hand	pond	
goal	coat	coal	

Dictation. Study these letters and words. Your teacher will dictate some of them.

e _____   f _____   o _____   b _____   j _____   a _____   i _____

m _____   c _____   p _____   g _____   a _____   p _____   h _____

Write these words.

mop _____   mope _____

cap _____   cape _____

pan _____   pane _____

pin _____   pine _____

10

Read the letters. Then write each letter several times. Write across the page from left to right.

Q $\quad$ Q Q ___

q $\quad$ q q ___

R $\quad$ R R ___

r $\quad$ r r ___

S $\quad$ S S ___

s $\quad$ s s ___

T $\quad$ T T ___

t $\quad$ t t ___

U $\quad$ U U ___

u $\quad$ u u ___

EXERCISE A

Read the letters. Circle the ones that are the same as the first letters, as in the example.

1. Uo uo (Uo) To
2. Qi qo Oi Qi
3. se ce sa se
4. tu tu vu ul
5. Re Se Re Ta
6. Ti Li Qi Ti

7. Pa Ba Pa Da
8. So So Ro Io
9. rr cc ee rr
10. Ui Di Ui Ci
11. qu ju gu qu
12. Sh Sh Ch Ds

EXERCISE B

Read the letters. Copy them after looking at the example.

Q ___ R ___ u ___ S ___ q ___ r ___ s ___ T ___

U ___ t ___ m ___ p ___ q ___ R ___ Q ___ b ___

EXERCISE C

Read the letters. Write them in alphabetical order, as in the example. When the first letter is the same, look at the next letter.

1. me   oa   da   na   _da me na oa_

2. qu   re   ti   sa   ___

3. je	ga	ru	li	_____
4. sl	sp	st	sq	_____
5. mi	ne	pr	qu	_____

EXERCISE D

Look at the pictures. Read the words, then write each word one time. Say the words and listen to the sounds.

sun   pup   rut   luck

round   hour   out   south

goat   roar   moan   soap

queen   quiet   quart

EXERCISE E

Put these words in alphabetical order, as in the example.

1. pond	hour	pane	hand	_hand hour pane pond_
2. coal	goal	cap	map	_____
3. dad	flag	run	queen	_____
4. dab	leaf	kick	deck	_____
5. mend	quiet	pan	out	_____

Read the letters. Then write each letter several times. Write across the page from left to right.

V V V _____
v v v _____
W W W _____
w w w _____
X X X _____
x x x _____
Y Y Y _____
y y y _____
Z Z Z _____
z z z _____

EXERCISE A

Listen to the teacher. The teacher will read two letters. Put a check mark (✓) next to them.

1. ua   va   ta
2. so   co   zo
3. ri   re   ra
4. wi   vi   ui

5. ye   te   le
6. za   xa   xe
7. to   bo   fo
8. zi   ze   xi

EXERCISE B

Read the letters. Check the letter or letters that are the same as the first letter. Look at the example.

1. b   d b p d b
2. y   g j y q y
3. v   v u c v w

4. z   c s r z s
5. W   m R W m
6. X   X Z N X

EXERCISE C

Read the letters, then write them. Look at the example.

v V   W ___   x ___   Z ___   X ___   w ___   Y ___   z ___
y ___   v ___   Z ___   x ___   v ___   u ___   y ___   U ___

EXERCISE D

Look at the pictures. Read the words, then write each word one time. Say the words and listen to the sounds.

van   vane   vine

write   wheel   whale

x-ray   exit   yield

zero   zebra   zoo

EXERCISE E

Read the words. Write them in alphabetical order.

sun	wheel	van	cape	pup	zero	zoo	hour
flag	roar	man	write	win	exit	yield	

_____

_____

_____

_____

_____

Dictation. Review the alphabet. Practice these letters and words. Your teacher will dictate some of them.

A a B b C c D d E e F f G g H h I i J j
K k L l M m N n O o P p Q q R r S s T t
U u V v W w X x Y y Z z

zoo   _zoo_   whale _whale_
vine _vine_   write _write_
zebra _zebra_   van   _van_
pine _pine_   pin   _pin_
cane _cane_   can   _can_

Cursive Alphabet

A a   B b   C c   D d   E e

F f   G g   H h   I i   J j

K k   L l   M m   N n   O o

P p   Q q   R r   S s   T t

U u   V v   W w   X x   Y y   Z z

My name is Susan

Smith. I am 20 years old.

I am from the United

States. I am a student at

the University of Arizona.

I live in an apartment.

Lesson 2
PERSONAL INFORMATION

Read this conversation. Complete the dialog by filling in the spaces.

Ellen: My name is Ellen Jensen. What's your name?

Student: *My name is* _____

Ellen: My family name is Jensen. What's yours?

Student: *My family name is* _____

Ellen: My first name is Ellen. What's yours?

Student: *My first name is* _____

Ellen: I am from the United States. Where are you from?

Student: *I am from* _____

PUNCTUATION

Here are some rules for punctuation.

.   Use a *period* at the end of a sentence.

?   Use a *question mark* at the end of a question.

'   Use an *apostrophe* in a contraction.
     I am = I'm
     What is = What's

Use a capital letter at the beginning of a sentence or question.

Use a capital letter for the pronoun *I*.

The names of people begin with a capital letter.

The names of countries begin with a capital letter.

EXERCISE A

Practice this information. Spell it correctly.

1. Write your family name two times.

   _____   _____

2. Write your first name two times.

   _____   _____

3. Write the name of your country.

   _____   _____

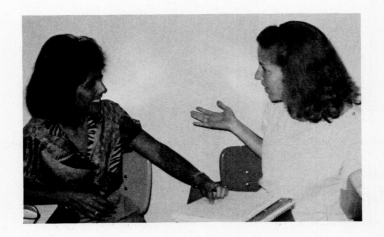

EXERCISE B

Copy the sentences two times. Say them. Learn to spell the words.

1. I don't understand.

_____

_____

2. I don't know.

_____

_____

3. Please repeat.

_____

_____

4. Please speak slowly.

_____

_____

5. Thank you.

_____

_____

EXERCISE C

Complete these words. Write one vowel in each space. Look at the example.

1. Pl e a s e r e p e a t.
2. Wh __ t's y __ __ r n __ m __?
3. Th __ nk y __ __.
4. Sp __ __ k sl __ wly.
5. __ d __ n't __ nd __ rst __ nd.
6. __ d __ n't kn __ w.

EXERCISE D

Read these conversations. Write one word in each space.

A: Good morning.
B: _Good_ _____.

A: What's your name?
B: _I'm sorry. I don't_ _____ _Please_ _____.

18

A: What's your name?

B: _My_____ is _____.

A: Where are you from?

B: _I'm from_____. Where are you from?_____.

A: I'm from Spain.

A: What's your first name?

B: _____.

A: What's your family name?

B: _My_____ name is_____.

GRAMMAR

Every sentence in English has a subject and verb.

(subject) (verb)
Ellen   is   from Spain.
(noun)

A pronoun takes the place of a noun.

She   is   from Spain.
(pronoun)

Pronouns and the Verb *to be*

I am	
You are	from Spain.
He She is It	

We You are They	from Spain.

Pronouns and the verb *to be* make *contractions*.

I am = I'm	we are = we're
you are = you're	you are = you're
he is = he's	they are = they're
she is = she's	
it is = it's	

Possessive Adjectives

My name Your name is His name Its name	easy to repeat.

Our names Your names are Their names	easy to repeat.

Dictation. **Learn to write these sentences. Your teacher will dictate them.**

1. *I don't understand.*
2. *I don't know.*
3. *Please repeat.*
4. *Please speak slowly.*
5. *Thank you.*
6. *My name is*
7. *I am from*

Lesson 3
DAYS OF THE WEEK

Write the correct days in these spaces.

Today is _____ (present time)
Tomorrow is _____ (future time)
Yesterday was _____ (past time)

monday
Tuesday
wednesday
Thursday
Friday
Saturday
Sunday

Punctuation: Capitalize the days of the week.

Copy the days of the week. Learn to spell them.

Monday   *Monday* _____

Tuesday   *Tuesday* _____

Wednesday	_Wednesday_
Thursday	_Thursday_
Friday	_Friday_
Saturday	_Saturday_
Sunday	_Sunday_

EXERCISE A

Write the answers to these questions.

1. What day is today?   _Today is_
2. What day is tomorrow?   _Tomorrow is_
3. What day was yesterday?   _Yesterday was_

EXERCISE B

Write the days of the week two times.

1. _____	1. _____
2. _____	2. _____
3. _____	3. _____
4. _____	4. _____
5. _____	5. _____
6. _____	6. _____
7. _____	7. _____

EXERCISE C

Abbreviations are short forms of words. Look at the abbreviations for the days of the week. Each one is followed by a period. Write the complete word for each abbreviation.

Mon.	_Monday_	Fri.	_____
Tues.	_____	Sat.	_____
Wed.	_____	Sun.	_____
Thurs.	_____		

EXERCISE D

Answer the questions. Write the complete word. Look at the examples.

1. What day comes after Sunday?   _Monday_
2. What day comes after Friday?   _____

3. What day comes before Thursday?   <u>Wednesday</u>

4. What day comes before Saturday?   _____

5. What day comes after Monday?   _____

6. What day comes after Tuesday?   _____

7. What day comes after Thursday?   _____

8. What day comes before Sunday?   _____

9. What day comes after Wednesday?   _____

10. What day comes before Tuesday?   _____

11. What day comes before Monday?   _____

12. What day comes before Wednesday?   _____

EXERCISE E

Complete the days. Fill in each space with one letter. Look at the example.

1. M <u>o</u> nd <u>a</u> <u>y</u>
2. _ ue _ _ ay
3. W _ _ nes _ _ _
4. _ hu _ _ d _ _

5. F _ id _ _
6. _ a _ urd _ _
7. Su _ _ ay
8. T _ _ s _ a _

EXERCISE F

These letters spell the days of the week. Unscramble them, and write the days of the week. Look at the example.

1. onmady   <u>Monday</u>
2. asudtrya   _____
3. ddywnsaee   _____
4. uarsyhtd   _____

5. iafdry   _____
6. useatdy   _____
7. uarsyhtd   _____
8. uaydns   _____

Dictation. Learn to write these letters, words, and sentences. The teacher will dictate some of them.

1. <u>My name is</u> _____
2. <u>I am from</u> _____
3. <u>I don't understand</u> _____
4. <u>Please speak slowly</u> _____

Sunday Monday Tuesday Wednesday Thursday Friday Saturday

b   d   g   p   y   h   m   n   a   e   s   c   z

yesterday   today   tomorrow   week   write   copy

Lesson 4
NUMBERS

Read these numbers. Write them.

0	zero	zero
1	one	one
2	two	two
3	three	three
4	four	four
5	five	five
6	six	six
7	seven	seven
8	eight	eight
9	nine	nine
10	ten	ten
11	eleven	eleven
12	twelve	twelve

13	thirteen	_thirteen_
14	fourteen	_fourteen_
15	fifteen	_fifteen_
16	sixteen	_sixteen_
17	seventeen	_seventeen_
18	eighteen	_eighteen_
19	nineteen	_nineteen_
20	twenty	_twenty_
21	twenty-one	_twenty-one_
30	thirty	_thirty_
40	forty	_forty_
50	fifty	_fifty_
60	sixty	_sixty_
70	seventy	_seventy_
80	eighty	_eighty_
90	ninety	_ninety_
100	one hundred	_one hundred_
1,000	one thousand	_one thousand_
1,000,000	one million	_one million_

Punctuation: Use a comma to separate thousands.
1,000,000

Read the numbers. Learn to write the numbers. Write each number several times.
Write across the page from left to right.

0	0	0
1	1	1
2	2	2
3	3	3
4	4	4
5	5	5
6	6	6
7	7	7

8	*8*	8
9	*9*	9
10	*10*	10

EXERCISE A

Read the number words. Write them as numbers. Look at the example.

1. fifty _50_
2. eighty-seven _____
3. one _____
4. ninety _____
5. fourteen _____
6. seventy _____

7. thirty _____
8. nineteen _____
9. sixty-six _____
10. one hundred _____
11. thirteen _____
12. twelve _____

EXERCISE B

Complete these numbers. Fill in each space with one letter. Then write the number. Look at the example.

1. fo _u_ r _4_
2. ___ in ___ t ___ ___ n _____
3. t ___ o _____
4. s ___ xt ___ ___ n _____
5. ___ ift ___ en _____
6. ___ w ___ l ___ e _____
7. o ___ e _____
8. t ___ e ___ ty _____
9. e ___ g ___ t _____
10. e ___ e ___ e ___ _____

11. s ___ v ___ nt ___ _____
12. ___ ix ___ y _____
13. th ___ r ___ ___ _____
14. n ___ n ___ ty _____
15. o ___ e th ___ ___ sand _____
16. o ___ e h ___ ndr ___ d _____
17. f ___ rty _____
18. ___ w ___ nty _____
19. ei ___ ___ ty _____
20. f ___ f ___ y _____

EXERCISE C

Listen to the teacher. The teacher will read one number in each group. Circle it.

1. 22   32   42
2. 56   55   15
3. 62   61   72
4. 17   70   71
5. 13   31   30

6. 500   502   532
7. 292   282   219
8. 127   134   123
9. 1,003   1,234   1,002
10. 1,041   1,040   1,014

EXERCISE D

Repeat Exercise C. The teacher will read a different number. Put a check (✓) above it.

EXERCISE E

Look at these problems. Read them, and write the answers.

+ plus   − minus   × times

1.	32	2.	657	3.	82	4.	55	5.	6,012
	+14		−103		−38		×11		−395

6.	72	7.	974	8.	5,128	9.	899	10.	14
	× 4		− 89		− 679		−437		× 7

Dictation. Write the numbers your teacher reads. Practice writing both the numbers and words.

_____   _____   _____
_____   _____   _____
_____   _____   _____
_____   _____   _____
_____   _____   _____

EXERCISE F

Many numbers are important. We use telephone numbers, addresses, and zip codes every day. Read these numbers.

Telephone numbers.

327-4902   298-7321   428-7301   624-5930   792-4110

Addresses. Look at these abbreviations. N. = North   S. = South
E. = East   W. = West   St. = Street   Ave. = Avenue

2942 N. Columbus   143 S. Main St.   1139 E. Speedway
329 W. Congress   2032 N. Broadway   47 N. Pine Ave.

Zip Codes.   Every address in the United States has a zip code. It helps the mail move faster. Read these zip codes.

85731   92506   62904   73416   10019

EXERCISE G

Answer the questions.

1. What is your telephone number? _____

2. What is your address? _____

_____

3. What is your zip code? _____

Now ask your classmates the same questions. Complete the chart with the information they give you.

NAME	TELEPHONE	ADDRESS	ZIP CODE

EXERCISE H

Listen to the teacher. The teacher will read one number in each row. Circle it.

1. 85,716   85,760   85,717
2. 3,480   4,308   3,408

3.	thirteen	thirty	thirty-three
4.	392	329	319
5.	325-6890	326-6981	325-9680
6.	15	50	51
7.	sixty	six	sixteen
8.	eleven	twelve	twenty
9.	299-0432	298-3042	298-4032
10.	734	34	634

EXERCISE I

Repeat exercise H. The teacher will read a different number. Put a check above it.

EXERCISE J

Look at the two columns of numbers. Match the numbers on the left with the words on the right, as in the example.

1.	4	twelve
2.	16	twenty
3.	12	sixteen
4.	30	thirty
5.	20	four

Punctuation. Use a decimal point between dollars and cents. Do not use a comma for a decimal point.

$4.25   four dollars and twenty-five cents
$4,250   four thousand two hundred and fifty dollars

EXERCISE K

These prices are in dollars and cents. Write them in words. Look at the example.

1. $1,389.38 _one thousand three hundred eighty-nine dollars and thirty-eight cents_

2. $279.00 _____

_____

3. $78.49 _____

_____

4. $1,090.16 _____

_____

5. $13.75 _____

_____

Dictation. Learn to write these numbers, words, and sentences. Your teacher will dictate some of them.

1. Write your name. _____

2. Write your address. _____

3. Review the numbers on page 24 . _____

4. Learn these words from the lesson.

    number   address   telephone   left   right

A paragraph is a group of sentences. Indent the first line of a paragraph. Look at these sentences about Mitsuo. Write them. Indent.

    Mitsuo is my friend. His address is 719 E. Main Street. He lives in an apartment. His telephone number is 795–3640.

Lesson 5
MONTHS

JANUARY	FEBRUARY	MARCH

S	M	T	W	TH	F	S		S	M	T	W	TH	F	S		S	M	T	W	TH	F	S
			1	2	3	4								1								1
5	6	7	8	9	10	11		2	3	4	5	6	7	8		2	3	4	5	6	7	8
12	13	14	15	16	17	18		9	10	11	12	13	14	15		9	10	11	12	13	14	15
19	20	21	22	23	24	25		16	17	18	19	20	21	22		16	17	18	19	20	21	22
26	27	28	29	30	31			23	24	25	26	27	28			23	24	25	26	27	28	29
																30	31				

APRIL	MAY	JUNE

S	M	T	W	TH	F	S		S	M	T	W	TH	F	S		S	M	T	W	TH	F	S
		1	2	3	4	5						1	2	3		1	2	3	4	5	6	7
6	7	8	9	10	11	12		4	5	6	7	8	9	10		8	9	10	11	12	13	14
13	14	15	16	17	18	19		11	12	13	14	15	16	17		15	16	17	18	19	20	21
20	21	22	23	24	25	26		18	19	20	21	22	23	24		22	23	24	25	26	27	28
27	28	29	30					25	26	27	28	29	30	31		29	30	31				

JULY	AUGUST	SEPTEMBER

S	M	T	W	TH	F	S		S	M	T	W	TH	F	S		S	M	T	W	TH	F	S
		1	2	3	4	5							1	2			1	2	3	4	5	6
6	7	8	9	10	11	12		3	4	5	6	7	8	9		7	8	9	10	11	12	13
13	14	15	16	17	18	19		10	11	12	13	14	15	16		14	15	16	17	18	19	20
20	21	22	23	24	25	26		17	18	19	20	21	22	23		21	22	23	24	25	26	27
27	28	29	30	31				24	25	26	27	28	29	30		28	29	30				
								31														

OCTOBER	NOVEMBER	DECEMBER

S	M	T	W	TH	F	S		S	M	T	W	TH	F	S		S	M	T	W	TH	F	S
			1	2	3	4								1			1	2	3	4	5	6
5	6	7	8	9	10	11		2	3	4	5	6	7	8		7	8	9	10	11	12	13
12	13	14	15	16	17	18		9	10	11	12	13	14	15		14	15	16	17	18	19	20
19	20	21	22	23	24	25		16	17	18	19	20	21	22		21	22	23	24	25	26	27
26	27	28	29	30	31			23	24	25	26	27	28	29		28	29	30	31			
								30														

Say the months of the year. Practice writing each month, and learn the abbreviations. Note that some months have no abbreviation.

Punctuation.   Use a period after an abbreviation. The name of each month begins with a capital letter.

Jan.	January	_Jan. January_
Feb.	February	_____
Mar.	March	_____
Apr.	April	_____
May	May	_____
June	June	_____
July	July	_____
Aug.	August	_____
Sept.	September	_____
Oct.	October	_____
Nov.	November	_____
Dec.	December	_____

EXERCISE A

1. Write the months that begin with J.

_____

2. Write the months that begin with M and N.

_____

3. Write the months that begin with A.

_____

EXERCISE B

Complete these sentences. Fill each space with the name of a month.

1. This month is _____ .   (present time)

2. Last month was _____ .   (past time)

3. Next month is _____ .   (future time)

EXERCISE C

Complete these months. Fill in each space with one letter. Then write the abbreviation for the months. Remember to use a period. Look at the examples.

1. M a r c h   _Mar._   13. _ pr _ _   _____
2. J u l y   _July_   14. _ ay   _____
3. J _ _ ua _ y _____   15. _ eb _ _ a _ y _____
4. S _ p _ e _ b _ r _____   16. _ u _ y   _____
5. M _ _   _____   17. _ ov _ _ b _ r _____
6. D _ c _ m _ er _____   18. _ an _ _ ry   _____
7. F _ b _ _ _ ry _____   19. _ ar _ _   _____
8. N _ v _ m _ e _ _____   20. _ ept _ _ ber   _____
9. J _ _ e   _____   21. _ ec _ _ ber   _____
10. O _ t _ _ e _ _____   22. _ u _ e   _____
11. A _ r _ l   _____   23. _ ug _ st   _____
12. A _ g _ s _   _____   24. _ ct _ ber   _____

DATES

We sometimes use numbers to write dates. In the United States, the first number is for the month, the middle number is for the day, and the last number is for the year. For example, 10/6/85 is October 6, 1985.

Punctuation. Use a comma between the day and the year. August 5, 1986.

EXERCISE D

Look at these dates, then read them aloud. Now write the complete dates after looking at the example.

1. 6/20/70   _June 20, 1970_   6. 4/30/47   _____
2. 10/17/51 _____   7. 11/21/29 _____
3. 2/26/74   _____   8. 7/15/64   _____
4. 12/11/83 _____   9. 1/19/81   _____
5. 5/31/87   _____   10. 3/12/48   _____

EXERCISE E

The dates on the left are of some important American holidays. Read each one and write the complete date. Then match that date with the name of the holiday, as in the example. If you do not know the holidays, ask your friends or your teacher.

1/1	*January first*	Independence Day
4/1	_____	Christmas
7/4	_____	New Year's Day
12/25	_____	Valentine's Day
2/14	_____	Thanksgiving

Fourth Thursday in November   April Fool's Day

First Monday in September   Labor Day

EXERCISE F

These are checks from the bank. Look at check number 1936. Look at the date and the names on the check. Look at the numbers. Fill in the spaces on check numbers 1937 and 1938.

```
TALIB P. STUDENT                                    1936
4516 E. Speedway Blvd.
Tucson, Arizona 85712                         91-2/1221
      325-7890                      September 6  19 85
Pay to the
order of  University Bookstore            $ 39.80
Thirty nine and eighty 100 ——————— Dollars
NATIONAL BANK  Speedway Office
 P.O. Box 123  Tucson, Arizona 85764

memo Textbook          Signed Talib P. Student
    "1:122100024:6785--3465"
```

```
TALIB P. STUDENT                                    1937
4516 E. Speedway Blvd.
Tucson, Arizona 85712                         91-2/1221
      325-7890                      _____  19 ___
Pay to the
order of _____  $ _____
_____ Dollars
NATIONAL BANK  Speedway Office
 P.O. Box 123  Tucson, Arizona 85764

                          Signed _____
memo _____
    "1:122100024:6785--3465"
```

```
TALIB  P.  STUDENT                                    1938
4516  E.  Speedway Blvd.               91-2/1221
Tucson, Arizona 85712
        325-7890              _____  19_____
Pay to the
order of _____  $ _____
_____  Dollars

NATIONAL BANK  Speedway Office
P.O. Box 123   Tucson, Arizona  85764

                       Signed _____
memo_____
      "1 :122100247:6785--3465 "
```

The Verb *to have*

I You have	a book.
He She has It	

We You	have	books.
They		

There is a poem in English that almost everyone learns. It helps us to remember how many days there are in each month.

> Thirty days hath September, April, June, and November.
> All the rest have thirty-one,
> Save February alone, which has twenty-eight
> Until Leap Year brings it twenty-nine.

The poem means this:

> September, April, June, and November have thirty days.
> All the other months have thirty-one days.
> February has 28 days.
> February has 29 days in a Leap Year.
> A Leap Year comes every four years.
> It has 366 days.

Punctuation. Use a comma after words in a list. September, April, June, and November have thirty days.

EXERCISE G

Complete these sentences by filling in each space with *have* or *has*. Look at the examples.

1. February _has_ twenty-eight days.

2. March and May _have_ thirty-one days.

3. September, April, June, and November _____ thirty days.

4. In Leap Year, Feb. _____ twenty-nine days.

5. August _____ thirty-one days.

6. December and January _____ thirty-one days.

7. All the rest of the months _____ thirty-one days.

ARIES March 21 - April 19	TAURUS April 20 - May 20	GEMINI May 21 - June 21	CANCER June 22 - July 22
LEO July 23 - August 22	VIRGO August 23 - September 22	LIBRA September 23 - October 23	SCORPIO October 24 - November 21
SAGITTARIUS November 22 - December 21	CAPRICORN December 22 - January 19	AQUARIUS January 20 - February 18	PISCES February 19 - March 20

EXERCISE H

Answer these questions. Write short answers.

1. What year were you born? _____

2. When is your birthday? _____

3. What is your zodiac sign? _____

Now ask your classmates these questions. Complete the chart. Do not use abbreviations for the months.

NAME	YEAR	BIRTHDAY	ZODIAC SIGN

EXERCISE I

Write the months of the year in order. Spell them correctly. Remember to capitalize the first letter of each month.

1. _____   7. _____

2. _____   8. _____

3. _____   9. _____

4. _____   10. _____

5. _____   11. _____

6. _____   12. _____

Dictation. Read the following sentences, then complete them by filling in the spaces with the correct words. Your teacher will dictate something similar.

_____ is my friend. She is _____ years old. She was born in _____

(year). Her birthday is on _____ (month/day). Her sign is _____.

Lesson 6
THE WEATHER

EXERCISE A

Look at the pictures. Read the sentences about the weather, then copy them.

1. How is the weather? The sun is shining. The girl is hot.

_____

_____

_____

2. How is the weather? It is snowing. It is cold. They are building a snowman.

_____

_____

_____

3. How is the weather? It is raining today. The man is wet. He is running.

_____

_____

_____

4. How is the weather? The wind is blowing now. It is windy. It is cold.

_____

_____

_____

_____

The Present Continuous tells about now. Expressions of time are *now, today, this week,* and *this year.*

be   +   verb(ing)

I	am	
You	are	running.
He		
She	is	
It		

We		
You	are	running.
They		

Use the verb *to be* + the *ing* form of the verb to make the present continuous.

EXERCISE B

Look at each picture below. Then write two sentences about it.

1. _____

_____

_____

2. _____

_____

_____

3. _____

_____

_____

4. _____

_____

_____

spring   summer   fall   winter

There are twelve months in each year. There are four seasons in each year. They are winter, spring, summer, and fall.

Punctuation. The names of the seasons are not capitalized.

EXERCISE C

Fill in each space with the name of a season. Look at the example.

1. July is in the   _summer_____ .
2. April is in the   _____ .
3. January is in the   _____ .
4. October is in the   _____ .
5. August is in the   _____ .
6. December is in the   _____ .

SPELLING

Double the last consonant of these verbs before you add *ing*.

swim + ing	swimming
run + ing	running
sit + ing	sitting

Drop the final *e* before you add *ing* to these verbs.

write + ing	writing
make + ing	making

EXERCISE D

Look at the pictures above. Then write one sentence about each. Use the present continuous. Look at the example.

1. _She is swimming._
2. _____
3. _____
4. _____

5. _____

6. _____

7. _____

8. _____

9. _____

10. _____

11. _____

12. _____

13. _____

14. _____

15. _____

16. _____

17. _____

EXERCISE E

Spelling Practice. Complete these words. Fill in each space with one letter. Look at the example.

1. r u n   ru n n ing   7. pla __   pl __ y __ __ __

2. s __ t   s __ t __ ing   8. m __ ke   m __ k __ n __

3. g __   g __ i __ g   9. __ t __ dy   s __ ud __ i __ __

4. b __ y   b __ y __ ng   10. __ __ ink   dr __ nk __ __ __

5. sw __ m   sw __ m __ ing   11. fl __   __ __ ying

6. sl __ __ p   __ __ ee __ ing   12. wr __ t __   wr __ t __ ng

Dictation. Look around your classroom. With your teacher and classmates, write a paragraph containing five or six sentences. Describe what people in your class are doing now. Use the present continuous. Remember to indent. Your teacher will dictate something similar.

_____

_____

_____

_____

_____

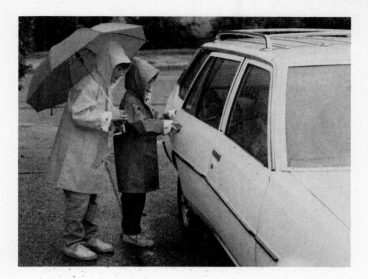

Writing Practice.   Look at the photo above. Write a paragraph about it. Remember to indent. Do not number the sentences. Here are some words you can use.

rain	cold wear	raincoat	long pants
hold	umbrella	open	door
car	go		

_____

_____

_____

_____

_____

_____

Lesson 7
ACTION!

Dr. and Mrs. Newman are in the living room. They always sit in the living room after dinner. They usually drink coffee. Tonight, they are sitting on the couch. They are reading a magazine. They are talking about a picture in the magazine. They often talk together.

EXERCISE A

Look at the picture and the sentences above. Then read the sentences in this exercise. Fill in each space with the correct word. Look at the example.

Dr. and Mrs. Newman are in the living room. They always _____ in the living room after dinner. They usually _____ coffee. Tonight, they are _____ on the couch. They are _____ a magazine. They are _____ about a picture in the magazine. They often _____ together.

ADVERBS OF FREQUENCY

Always, usually, often, sometimes, rarely, and *never* are *adverbs of frequency*. They tell how often something happens.

always	=	100% of the time
usually	=	80% +
often	=	75% +
sometimes	=	30% +
rarely	=	10% −
never	=	0%

Write adverbs of frequency after the verb *to be*.

It is *always* hot here in the summer.

It is *never* hot in the winter.

The simple present makes statements of fact or tells what usually happens.

Simple Present

I You		swim	
He She It	often	swims	in the summer.
We You They	often	swim	in the summer.

SPELLING

When the verb ends in *y* preceded by a consonant, change the *y* to *i* and add *es*.

study	studies	buy	buys
fly	flies	say	says
try	tries	play	plays

Some verbs are irregular. Add *es* to these verbs.

go	goes
do	does
teach	teaches

EXERCISE B

Spelling Practice. Complete these words, putting one letter in each space. Look at the example.

1. st <u>u</u> d <u>y</u>   st <u>u</u> d <u>i</u> <u>e</u> <u>s</u>   6. pl __ y   pl __ y __

2. t __ __ ch   t __ __ ch __ __   7. s __ y   s __ y __

3. b __ y   b __ y __   8. g __   g __ __ s

4. d __   d __ __ s   9. fl __   fl __ __ s

5. __ __ udy   st __ d __ __ __   10. d __   d __ __ s

EXERCISE C

Read these sentences. Fill in each space with the simple present form of the verb. Use the verb at the end of the sentence. Look at the examples.

1. His family ___goes___ on vacation in the summer. (go)

2. Many people ___ski___ in the winter. (ski)

3. My sister usually _____ in the summer. (swim)

4. Children often _____ lemonade in the summer. (drink)

5. Many families _____ on picnics in the spring. (go)

6. People usually _____ football in the fall. (play)

7. Children sometimes _____ hot chocolate in the winter. (drink)

8. My brothers _____ in the spring. (run)

9. Children _____ to school in the fall, winter, and spring. (go)

10. My roommate usually _____ to school in the summer. (go)

EXERCISE D

Look at the pictures on the calendar in Figure 7–1. Write a sentence about Gloria for each day of the week. Look at the example.

1. Gloria

2. Gloria _____ on Tuesday.

3. Gloria _____ .

4. _____ on Thursday.

5. _____

6. _____ .

7. _____ Sunday.

FIGURE 7-1

Dictation.   With your teacher and classmates, write a paragraph of five or six sentences about your daily classroom routine. Then your teacher will dictate something similar. Remember to indent.

_____

_____

_____

_____

_____

_____

_____

_____

Writing Practice A.   Write five to seven sentences about the weather where you are living now. Tell about the seasons. Indent the first sentence.

_____

_____

_____

_____

_____

_____

_____

Writing Practice B.   Look at the photo below. Write five to seven sentences about it. Indent the first sentence. Here are some words you can use.

| office | flower | window blinds |
| desk | bookshelves | |

_____

_____

_____

_____

_____

_____

_____

Lesson 8
FAMILY

Paul and Mary are married. They have four children. They have two sons and two daughters. Their sons are Tom and Bill. Their daughters are Linda and Sara.

This is Paul.
He is 48 years old.
He is tall.

This is Mary.
She is 46 years old.
She is short.

Bill
13

Tom
15

Sara
17

Linda
22

Sam
25

single
not married

Alice
one year old

FIGURE 8-1 The Atkinson family

PLURAL NOUNS

Add *s* to form the plural of nouns.

1 cousin	3 cousin*s*
1 son	2 son*s*
1 aunt	4 aunt*s*

Some plurals are irregular. Learn these plurals. Do not add *s* to them.

1 child	6 children
1 man	3 men
1 woman	5 women

EXERCISE A

Read the sentences. Fill in each space with *child, children, man, men, woman* or *women*. Look at the example.

1. Linda has one _child_ .
2. The _____ are tall.
3. Tom and Bill are _____ .
4. Linda and Sara are _____ .
5. Mr. Atkinson has four _____ .
6. How many _____ do Paul and Mary have?

FAMILY VOCABULARY

father	mother	son	daughter
brother	sister	uncle	aunt
husband	wife	nephew	niece
cousin	cousin	grandfather	grandmother

A AND AN

Use *a* with singular nouns. *An* is the same as *a*. Use *a* before a consonant and *an* before a vowel.

My friend is *a* doctor.
My brother is *an* engineer.
My uncles are dentists.

Do not use *a* or *an* with plural nouns.

EXERCISE B

Look at the pictures of the Atkinson family on page 49. Talk about family relationships with your teacher. Read the sentences and fill in the blanks with a singular or plural noun, as in the examples.

1. Bill and Tom are _brothers_ .
2. Linda has one _sister_ .
3. Linda has two _____ .
4. Alice has an _____ .
5. Linda and Sara are _____ .
6. Bill and Tom are _____ .
7. Paul and Mary have four _____ .
8. Sam has a _____ .

9. Sam and Linda have one _____ .

10. Sara, Tom, and Bill have one _____ .

Negative of the Verb *to be*

I'm You're He's She's It's	not	hungry.

We're You're They're	not	hungry.

You He She It	aren't isn't	hungry.

We You They	aren't	hungry.

Questions with the Verb *to be*

Am	I	
Are	you	
Is	he she it	hungry?

Are	we you they	hungry?

EXERCISE C

Read these sentences. Look at the pictures of the Atkinson family on page 49. Fill in each space with one word. Use the verb *to be* or the negative of *to be*, as in the examples.

1. Linda and Alice _aren't_ sisters.

2. Tom and Bill _are_ brothers.

3. Sara and Linda _____ their sisters.

4. Mary and Paul _____ married.

5. Alice _____ one year old.

6. Bill _____ married.

7. Tom _____ single.

8. Linda and Sam _____ married.

9. Linda _____ his wife.

10. Tom _____ 15 years old.

11. Bill _____ 15 years old.

POSSESSIVE

Add *'s* to make the singular possessive.

write this	do not write this
Alice's brother	= the brother of Alice
Linda's father	= the father of Linda

Add *'* to make the plural possessive.

| the boys' father | = the father of the boys |
| the girls' brother | = the brother of the girls |

Add *'s* for irregular plural nouns.

| the women's father | = the father of the women |
| the children's aunt | = the aunt of the children |

EXERCISE D

Look at the pictures of the Atkinson family and read these sentences. Fill in each space with one word, as in the examples.

1. Paul is Linda's   _father_   .
2. Tom is Alice's   _uncle_   .
3. Bill is Tom's   _____   .
4. Mary is Bill's   _____   .
5. Linda is Tom's   _____   .
6. Mary is Alice's   _____   .
7. Paul is Linda's   _____   .
8. Sam is Linda's   _____   .

Punctuation.   Use an apostrophe with the possessive.

EXERCISE E

Read the sentences. Add *'s* if necessary. Some sentences do not need it. Look at the examples.

1. Alice _____ is one year old.
2. Mary is Linda 's_____ mother.
3. Mary is Paul _____ wife.
4. Linda and Sam _____ are married.
5. Bill and Tom _____ are men.
6. Bill and Tom are Paul _____ sons.
7. Linda _____ is a woman.
8. Bill is Tom _____ brother.
9. Sara is Alice _____ aunt.
10. Linda is Sam _____ wife.
11. Linda and Sam _____ are married.
12. Their daughter _____ name is Alice.

EXERCISE F

Look at the photo above. Name the people and describe the family relationships you see. Write five to seven sentences about the picture. Indent the first sentence.

_____
_____
_____
_____
_____
_____

54

Use *do* and *does* in the negative and with questions for the simple present tense.

Do and Does

I you	don't	
He She It	doesn't	have an airplane.

We You They		don't have an airplane.

Do	I you	
Does	he she it	have an airplane?

Do	we you they	have an airplane?

EXERCISE G

Read the questions. Fill in each space with *do* or *does.* Look at the examples.

1. _Do_ you have a sister?
2. _Does_ Tom have a cousin?
3. _____ they drink lemonade in the summer?
4. _____ he have two brothers?
5. _____ she swim in a big pool?
6. _____ it rain in the spring?
7. _____ you have a large family?
8. _____ you have any brothers?

EXERCISE H

Read the sentences. Fill in each space with *don't* or *doesn't.* Look at the examples.

1. My roommate _doesn't_ have a house.
2. Sara and Will _don't_ have any children.
3. Ellen _____ drink coffee.
4. It _____ usually snow in summer.
5. We _____ study French.
6. My roommate and I _____ work here.

EXERCISE I

Read each line. One word is different from the others. Draw a circle around it. Look at the example.

1. January   March   (Tuesday)   April
2. sister   brother   map   son
3. Mexico   Saudi Arabia   Sudan   son
4. spring   student   summer   fall
5. aunt   grandfather   son   uncle
6. Monday   September   Saturday   Wednesday
7. sixty   eighty   thirty   fourteen
8. A   C   b   D

Writing Practice A. Describe your family in five to seven sentences. Indent the first sentence.

_____

_____

_____

_____

_____

_____

Writing Practice B. Look at the picture above. Write five to seven sentences about it. Indent the first sentence.

_____

_____

_____

_____

_____

_____

56

Lesson 9
OCCUPATIONS

FIGURE 9–1

EXERCISE A

Look at the pictures in Figure 9-1. Read the sentences. Fill in each space with the correct form of the verb *to be.* Look at the examples.

1. He __isn't__ an engineer. He __is__ a student.
2. He _____ a dentist. He _____ a lawyer.
3. They _____ secretaries. They _____ engineers.
4. She _____ a nurse. She _____ a secretary.
5. My friend _____ a lawyer. He _____ a businessman.
6. He _____ a student. He _____ a teacher.
7. They _____ businessmen. They _____ ranchers.
8. She _____ a lawyer. She _____ a dentist.
9. I _____ a _____ . I _____ .
10. My brother _____ . He _____ .
11. My father _____ . He _____ .
12. My mother _____ . She _____ .

EXERCISE B

This will help you with spelling. Look at each word. Then cover the word and write it on the next line. Look at the typed word again and check your spelling. Then practice it some more.

doctor   student   teacher

doctor _____

_____

_____

secretary   businessman   dentist

_____

_____

_____

uncle   aunt   cousin

_____

_____

_____

friend   engineer   brother

_____

_____

_____

_____

EXERCISE C

Read the sentences. If necessary, fill in each space with *a* or *an*. Some sentences do not need it. Look at the examples.

1. My roommate's sisters are _____ nurses.

2. John is ___an___ engineer.

3. My mother is _____ teacher.

4. Her friends' sisters are _____ secretaries.

5. Their teachers are _____ women.

6. I see _____ dentist every six months.

7. The man is _____ policeman.

8. Our teacher is _____ English teacher.

9. Glen's brothers are _____ ranchers.

10. My daughter is _____ student.

EXERCISE D

Look at the groups of words. Write a complete sentence with each group, as in the example.

1. Joe's uncle/rancher

    Joe's uncle is a rancher. _____

2. his brothers/engineers

    _____

3. his father/policeman

    _____

4. his father/not/student

    _____

5. his aunts/lawyers

    _____

EXERCISE E

Write five sentences about your family. Tell about their occupations.

1. _____
2. _____
3. _____
4. _____
5. _____

1. There is a salesperson in the store.
2. There is an architect in the office.
3. There are two mechanics in the garage.
4. There are two housewives in the kitchen.

60

EXERCISE F

Read the sentences. Fill in each space with *There is* or *There are.* Use *There is* with the singular, and *There are* with the plural. Look at the examples.

1. _There is_____ a student in the cafeteria.
2. _There are_____ three policemen in the car.
3. _____ a salesperson in the store.
4. _____ a businessman in the office.
5. _____ two ranchers in the truck.
6. _____ two architects in the house.
7. _____ one teacher in the classroom.
8. _____ students in this class.

SOME AND ANY

Use *any* in questions and in the negative. Use *some* with affirmative.
    Are there *any* students in the room?
        Yes, there are some students in the room.
        Yes, there are fifteen students in Dena's class.
    Are there *any* nurses in the office?
        No, there aren't *any* nurses in the office.

EXERCISE G

Look at the groups of words. Write a complete sentence with each group, as in the example.

1. doctors/my friend's family
   _There are two doctors in my friend's family._____

2. not/students/store

   _____

3. women/our class

   _____

4. engineers/my family

   _____

5. policeman/building/now

   _____

6. mechanics/our class

   _____

7. secretaries/the office

_____

8. housewives/our class

_____

9. not/nurses/garage

_____

10. ranchers/shop

_____

Can shows ability. Use the simple verb after *can*. *Can* does not change.

Can

I You He She It We You They	can walk fast.

EXERCISE H

Read the sentences and fill in each space with a verb. Look at the example.

1. My sister is a doctor. She can _examine the baby_ .
2. My father is an architect. He can _____ .
3. Rick is a teacher. He can _____ .
4. Sara is an engineer. She can _____ .
5. My nephew is a student. He can _____ .

Dictation. With your teacher and classmates, write a paragraph of four or five sentences about your classmates. Tell about their occupations. Remember to indent. Your teacher will dictate something similar.

_____

_____

_____

_____

_____

Writing Practice. Look at the photo in Figure 9–2. Write a paragraph about it in five to seven sentences. Remember to indent. Here are some words you can use.

department store	clothes	dresses	salesperson
customer	show	wheelchair	

_____

_____

_____

_____

_____

_____

_____

_____

FIGURE 9–2

Lesson 10
ILLNESS

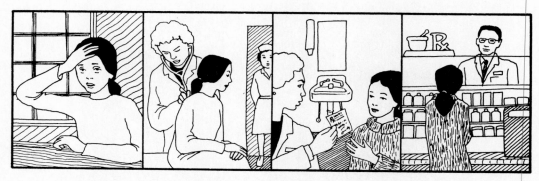

My friend Nancy was sick last night. She had a fever of 101°F. She was very tired. She was coughing and sneezing. She went to the doctor. The doctor examined her. He gave her a prescription for some medicine. She went to the drugstore and bought the medicine.

Past of *to be* and *to have*

I was	
You were	sick yesterday.
He She was It	

We You were They	sick yesterday.

I You He She had We You They	a cold two days ago.

VOCABULARY

Look at these sentences.

Nancy was _____ last night. She had a _____ .

sick	fever
tired	headache
coughing	stomachache
sneezing	sore throat

EXERCISE A

Read the questions and answer them. Look at the example.

1. Was Nancy sick?   _Yes, she was._

    What was wrong?   _She was_ _____ sick.

                        She had _____ a headache.

                        _____ a fever.

2. Was George sick?   Yes, _____

    What was wrong?   _____ a fever.

                        _____ coughing.

                        _____ a stomachache.

3. Were you sick?   Yes, _____

    What was wrong?   _____ a sore throat.

                        _____ a headache.

                        _____ sneezing.

EXERCISE B

Read the questions and answer them. Look at the example.

1. What was wrong with Mary and Tom?

    They _were_ sick.

    They _____ coughing yesterday.

2. What was wrong with Helen?

    She _____ tired. She _____ a sore throat.

    She _____ sick.

3. What was wrong with you last week?

    I _____ a fever. I _____ coughing.

    I _____ a sore throat.

4. What was wrong with you and your roommate?

We _____ colds. We _____ fevers.

We _____ coughing and sneezing.

Writing Practice. Use the following words and write three or four sentences about these people. Indent the first sentence.

1. Ahmed   sick   fever   coughing   last Friday

_____

_____

_____

_____

2. Nadia   sore throat   sneezing   sick   yesterday

_____

_____

_____

3. Pablo   stomachache   sick   last Sunday

_____

_____

_____

4. Mark   tired   headache   sore throat   yesterday

_____

_____

_____

5. Lucy   fever   sick   earache   two weeks ago

_____

_____

_____

_____

PAST

Add *ed* to make the past tense of many verbs. If the verb ends in *e,* add only *d.*

need	needed	examine	examined
want	wanted	prescribe	prescribed

Many verbs are irregular. Learn these verbs.

have	had	go	went
do	did	eat	ate
buy	bought	give	gave
feel	felt	hurt	hurt
drink	drank	sleep	slept
write	wrote	sit	sat

Some expressions of time that indicate the past are *yesterday, last night, last weekend, last month,* and *a week ago.*

EXERCISE C

Read the sentences. Fill in each space with the past of the verb. Look at the example.

1. My grandfather _needed_ a car last year.   (need)

2. The sick child _____ for twelve hours yesterday.   (sleep)

3. My friend _____ sick last night.   (feel)

4. He _____ some medicine last night.   (need)

5. My ear _____ last night.   (hurt)

6. Ellen _____ some medicine two days ago.   (buy)

7. My sister _____ a stomachache last night.   (have)

8. My two friends _____ sick last week.   (be)

9. His daughter _____ a sore throat.   (have)

10. They _____ to the doctor.   (go)

11. The doctor _____ her some medicine.   (give)

12. They _____ the medicine at the drugstore.   (buy)

Questions in the Past with *did*

Did	I you he she It we you they	feel sick last weekend?

Negative in the Past with *did*

I You He She It We You They	did	not feel sick a week ago.

EXERCISE D

Read the sentences. They are in the present. Change them to the past. Use an expression of past time. Look at the example.

1. My friend doesn't need shampoo today.

   She bought shampoo yesterday.

2. Bill buys medicine every month.

   _____

3. My friend doesn't need a roommate now.

   _____

4. My sister isn't sick this week.

   _____

5. She goes to the doctor every week.

   _____

6. The doctor gives her a new prescription every year.

   _____

7. She feels good today.

   _____

8. The students don't have sore throats today.

   _____

9. I often buy cough medicine.

   _____

10. I don't have an earache.

    _____

COUNT AND NONCOUNT NOUNS

You can count many things: one pill, two pills.
Count nouns have singular and plural forms. Use *a* or *one* with the singular form of a count noun. Use *some* or a number with the plural form.

a prescription	two prescriptions	some prescriptions
a comb	five combs	some combs
a pill	twenty-five pills	some pills

You cannot count some things such as medicine and toothpaste. There is no plural form for these nouns. Use *some* or *nothing* with *noncount nouns.*

| medicine | some medicine | soap | some soap |
| toothpaste | some toothpaste | lotion | some lotion |

Dictation. Read these sentences. Fill in each space with one word to make complete sentences. Your teacher will dictate something similar.

Kevin was sick yesterday. He had a _____ . He needed _____ . He _____ to the drugstore. He bought _____ .

EXERCISE E

Read the sentences and fill in each space with *a* or *some.* Look at the examples.

1. Susan needed <u>some</u> shampoo yesterday.

2. Bill bought _____ comb.

3. Nancy and I bought _____ lotion.

4. Mr. Smith had _____ prescription.

5. Maria needed _____ brush.

6. Abdullah bought _____ toothpaste yesterday.

7. We needed _____ soap last week.

8. They bought _____ medicine at the drugstore last night.

Writing Practice A.   Write a paragraph of five to seven sentences about a trip to the drugstore. Tell what you needed and what you bought. Remember to indent.

_____

_____

_____

_____

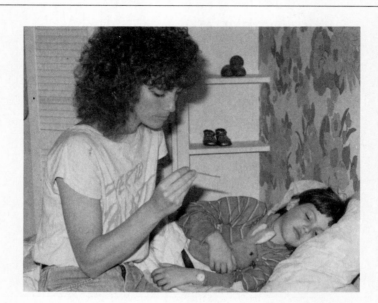

Writing Practice B. Look at the picture above. Write a story about it. Remember to indent. Here are some words you can use.

in bed   thermometer   toy

_____

_____

_____

_____

_____

_____

_____

_____

Review Exercises for Unit I

EXERCISE A

Supply the past form of each verb given in parentheses. Look at the example.

Mary _had_ (have) a headache. She _____ (feel) awful. She _____ (know) she should not go to school, but Mary _____ (go) to school anyway. On the way to school, Mary _____ (see) some friends. They _____ (be) surprised to see Mary. They _____ (know) Mary _____ (be) sick. They _____ (say), "Why don't you go home and rest?"

Mary _____ (say), "I _____ (think) about it, but I have so much work. I don't want to miss school."

In the afternoon Mary _____ (eat) a small lunch. She _____ (drink) a lot of water. By the time she _____ (come) home, Mary _____ (feel) better. Mary's roommate _____ (speak) to her. "I'm glad you feel better, Mary, because now we can go out."

Mary _____ (say) no because she _____ (have) a lot of homework. After she _____ (do) her homework, Mary _____ (sit) down and _____ (write) a letter to her friend in Mexico.

EXERCISE B

Read the conversation. Fill in each space with *some* or *a.*

A new student at school goes to the drugstore because she needs to buy many things. A saleswoman helps her.

Student: Excuse me. I am _____ new student here, and I have many things to buy. Can you help me?

Saleswoman: Of course. What do you need? I'll help you find everything.

Student: I need _____ toothpaste and _____ toothbrush.

Saleswoman: Here they are. Do you need _____ brush or _____ comb?

Student: No, but I need _____ soap and _____ lotion. I also need _____ shampoo.

Saleswoman: This is _____ good brand of shampoo. Use this.

Student: I also have an allergy. The doctor gave me _____ prescription for _____ pills.

Saleswoman: We can fill your prescription here.

Student: I had _____ medicine at home for my allergy, but I didn't bring it with me.

Saleswoman: Do you need anything else?

Student: No, thank you. You have been very helpful. How much do I owe you?

Saleswoman: That comes to seven dollars and forty-five cents.

Look at the picture above and write a story about it. Here are some words you can use.

chicken   picnic   park   baseball cap   grandson

_____

_____

_____

_____

_____

_____

_____

_____

_____

_____

_____

Unit II
Lesson 11

BUYING A CAR

Objectives of Unit II in order of importance:

  writing grammatical sentences
  joining sentences
  sequence of ideas
  punctuation
  vocabulary acquisition
  additional grammatical patterns

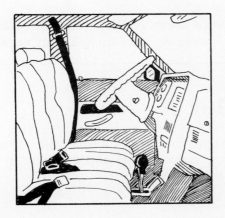

1. George does not have a car.
   He needs to go to work every day.
   He wants to buy a car.

2. He wants to buy a new car.
   He does not have enough money.
   He has $3,000.
   He has to buy a used car.

3. George is married.
   He has three children.
   He needs a big car.
   He does not want to buy a small car.
   He does not want to buy a truck, either.

4. He lives in the desert.
   It is very hot in the summer.
   He wants to have an air-conditioner.
   He also wants a radio.

5. George is looking at cars.
   He wants to look under the hood.
   He wants to look at the engine.

6. He wants to buy a station wagon.

7. George does not have enough money for the station wagon.
   He needs to borrow some money.
   He has to go to the bank.

8. He needs to borrow $2,000.
   He has to pay interest.
   He has to make monthly payments.

9. The family has a new car.
   Everyone is very happy.

USING TO *BEFORE A VERB*

These verbs use *to* before another verb.

want to	
need to	study
have to	
like to	

We often use expressions of future time with these verbs. Some expressions of future time are *tonight, tomorrow, next Thursday, next month, and next year.*

EXERCISE A

Read the sentences. Then fill in each space with the correct form of the verbs *want to, need to, have to,* or *like to.* Remember to put *s* on the end of the verb when the subject is he, she, or it. Look at the examples.

1. George does not have a car. He __wants to__ buy a car.
2. Sally does not have any money. She ___needs___ to borrow some from the bank.
3. George borrowed some money from the bank. He _____ pay interest.
4. He _____ make monthly payments.
5. Harry is sick. He _____ go to the doctor.
6. I did not eat breakfast. I _____ eat lunch.
7. Sara does not have any money. She _____ borrow some.
8. Bill is a carpenter. He _____ buy a truck.
9. The children like pizza. They _____ eat pizza.
10. Andrew has a test. He _____ study.

EXERCISE B

Read the sentences. Then fill in each space with the correct form of *have to* or *have*. Look at the examples.

1. George and Helen ___have___ a big family.
2. It is 8:30 A.M. Linda ___has to___ go to school.
3. It is dinner time. Bill and Nancy _____ go home.
4. My favorite color is blue. I _____ a blue car.
5. We received two letters last week. We _____ write some letters today.
6. Harry _____ three brothers.
7. I want to cash a check. I _____ go to the bank.
8. Sara borrowed money. She _____ pay interest.
9. The students _____ do their homework.
10. They _____ a lot of homework.
11. Lucy _____ $5,000.

EXERCISE C

Read the sentences, and fill in each space with the correct form of *want to* or *want*. Look at the examples.

1. George ___wants___ a car.
2. He ___wants to___ buy a used car.
3. He _____ $3,000.
4. He _____ borrow $3,000 from the bank.
5. Evelyn _____ a new house.

6. She _____ buy an apartment.

7. Harry _____ go to the movie tonight.

8. He _____ chicken for dinner tonight.

9. The children _____ go to the park.

10. The cat _____ eat.

BECAUSE

Because answers the question *why*. It gives the reason for something. Look at the examples.

   Jim wants a big car because he has a big family.

   He has to borrow money because he does not have enough.

EXERCISE D

Read the sentences. Then join them with *because*. Be sure to put the result first, and put the reason after *because*. First look at the examples.

1. George wants to buy a car.
   He needs to drive to work.

   <u>George wants to buy a car because he needs</u>
   <u>to drive to work.</u>

2. They want to buy an expensive car.
Tom and Linda have to borrow money from the bank.

<u>Tom and Linda have to borrow money from the
bank because they want to buy an expensive car.</u>

3. It is hot in Tucson in the summer.
They want a car with air conditioning.

_____

_____

4. I am hungry. I have to eat a sandwich.

_____

_____

5. He does not want to walk to work.
Bill needs to buy a car.

_____

_____

6. He has a big family. George needs a big car.

_____

_____

7. I need some money. I want to go to the bank.

_____

_____

8. I have to cash a check. I want to go to the bank.

_____

_____

9. He wants to see the engine.
George has to look under the hood.

_____

_____

10. He has a test tomorrow. Andrew has to study.

_____

_____

Dictation. With your teacher and classmates, write a paragraph about buying a
car. Remember to indent. Your teacher will dictate something similar.

_____

_____

_____

_____

Punctuation. Begin the names of people, countries, and cities with a capital letter.

EXERCISE E

Punctuation Practice.   Read these sentences about Evelyn and Alex, and punctuate them. Look at the example.

1. *E* evelyn and *A* alex want to buy a new house.

2. they work in new york city

3. they want to live outside new york

4. they want a small house because they dont have any children

5. they need to borrow money because the houses in new york city are very expensive

Writing Practice A. Make a list of things to do. For example:

study

call my parents

Using the information in your list, write some sentences, telling whether you *have to, need to,* or *want to* do them. Use expressions of time such as *next summer, next week, today,* and *later.*

Writing Practice B. Look at the picture in Figure 11–1. Write a story about it. Remember to indent. Here are some words you can use.

hood	price
used cars	loan
car lot	expensive
	cheap

FIGURE 11–1

Lesson 12
DEFENSIVE DRIVING

1. Drivers must have drivers' licenses.

2. Drivers must stop for red lights.
   They should stop for yellow lights.
   They should not run yellow lights.
   They can go on green lights.

3. Drivers must stop at stop signs.
   They should yield to the driver on the right.
   The driver on the right should go first.

4. Drivers can sometimes turn right on red lights.
   First, they must stop.
   They should signal to turn left or right.

5. All drivers should obey the speed limit.

6. All drivers should fasten their seat belts.

7. A driver must not pass a stopped school bus.

8. A driver must stop for pedestrians.
   Pedestrians should use the crosswalk.

9. Drivers should stop at railroad crossings.
   They must stop for trains.

10. Drivers must not drive fast.
    They should drive carefully.

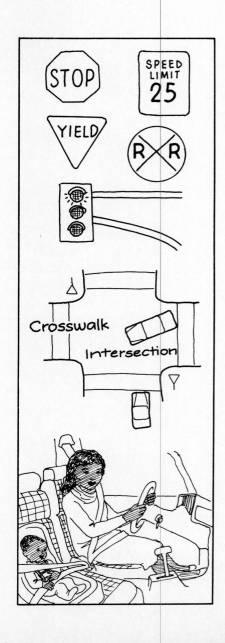

MUST / SHOULD

Must and *should* are different. *Must* has the same meaning as *have to.* You have no choice. For example, you must stop at a red light.

Should means that it is a good idea to do something. You have a choice and a responsibility. For example, you should cross the street at the crosswalk.

Should and *must* come before the verb. They do not change. The negatives are *should not* and *must not.*

EXERCISE A

Read the following sentences. Fill in each space with *must* or *should.* Either may be correct in some sentences. Be sure you can understand the difference. Look at the examples.

1. A driver _must_ have a driver's license.
2. A driver _should_ use a seat belt.
3. A good driver _____ drive safely.
4. A car _____ stop for a school bus.
5. A driver _____ slow down in a school zone.
6. A driver _____ stop for pedestrians.
7. A driver _____ signal before he turns.
8. A pedestrian _____ use the crosswalk.
9. People _____ drive carefully.
10. A good student _____ come to class every day.
11. A good student _____ do the homework.
12. A good student _____ practice every day.
13. A good student _____ work hard.
14. A good student _____ be on time for class.
15. A good student _____ study.

EXERCISE B

Read these sentences. Fill in the blanks with *should* or *should not.* Look at the examples.

1. A driver _should not_ pass another car on the right.
2. A driver _should_ obey the speed limit.
3. A driver _____ drive more than fifty-five miles per hour.
4. A driver _____ talk and drive at the same time.
5. A driver _____ always drive safely.

6. A student _____ always do the homework.

7. A student _____ talk when the teacher is talking.

8. A student _____ raise her hand when she wants to talk.

9. A student _____ say, "Excuse me" when he is late.

10. A student _____ leave the room in the middle of class.

Dictation. With your teacher and classmates, write a paragraph about safe drivers. Remember to indent. Your teacher will dictate something similar.

_____

_____

_____

_____

_____

_____

_____

EXERCISE C

Look at the phrases. Then write about *good drivers,* using the words *should* or *must,* as in the examples.

1. to turn right

   Good drivers should signal to turn right.

2. at a red light

   Good drivers must stop at a red light.

3. drive carefully

_____

4. the speed limit

_____

5. a driver's license

_____

6. use the seat belt

_____

7. to turn left

_____

8. for pedestrians

_____

EXERCISE D

Look at the phrases. Then write about a good student, using *should, must, should not,* and *must not,* as in the examples.

1. on time
   A good student should be on time.

2. be absent
   A good student should not be absent.

3. the homework

_____

4. be late for class

_____

5. practice every day

_____

6. study hard

_____

7. say, "Excuse me"

_____

8. talk in class to friends

_____

BEFORE, AFTER, WHEN

Before, after, and _when_ tell when something happens.

1   2
A good driver always signals _before_ she turns.

    1. the driver signals
    2. the driver turns

2   1
Many students buy cars _after_ they come to the U.S.

    1. the students come to the U.S.
    2. the students buy cars

You must pay a tax _when_ you buy a car in the U.S.
The two things happen at the same time.

EXERCISE E

Read the sentences. Then combine them to make one sentence. Use _before, after,_ or _when,_ as in the examples.

Getting a Driver's License

1. You should study the driver's book.
   You go to the Department of Motor Vehicles.

   You should study the driver's book before you go to the Department of Motor Vehicles.

2. You should take $5.00 with you.
   You go to the Department of Motor Vehicles.

   You should take $5.00 with you when you go to the Department of Motor Vehicles.

3. You should get in line.
   You get to the Department of Motor Vehicles.

   _____

   _____

4. You must pay your money.
   You show your old license.

   _____

   _____

5. You must fill out an application.
   You show your old license.

   _____

   _____

6. You must take a written test.
   You get a license.

   _____

   _____

7. You should answer the questions carefully.
   You take the written test.

   _____

   _____

8. You must take the eye examination.
   The officer takes your photograph.

   _____

   _____

9. You should stand still. You take your picture.

   _____

   _____

10. You must wait six or eight weeks.
    Your license will come in the mail.

    _____

    _____

EXERCISE F

See the driver's-license application form. Fill in the information about yourself.

```
┌────────────────────────────────────────────────────────────────┐
│            DRIVER'S  LICENSE  APPLICATION                        │
│  ┌──────────────────────────────────────────────────────────┐   │
│  │  FIRST  NAME      MIDDLE NAME        LAST NAME            │   │
│  │                                                           │   │
│  ├──────────────────────────────────────────────────────────┤   │
│  │  STREET                                                   │   │
│  │  ADDRESS                                                  │   │
│  ├──────────────────────────────────────────────────────────┤   │
│  │    CITY             STATE            ZIP CODE             │   │
│  │                                                           │   │
│  ├───────────────┬──────────┬──────────┬────────────────────┤   │
│  │  HAIR  COLOR  │  EYES    │  HEIGHT  │   WEIGHT           │   │
│  │               │          │          │                    │   │
│  ├───────────────┴──────────┴──────────┴────────────────────┤   │
│  │  DATE OF   MONTH   DAY   YEAR  │   TODAY'S  DATE          │   │
│  │  BIRTH                         │                          │   │
│  └──────────────────────────────────────────────────────────┘   │
└────────────────────────────────────────────────────────────────┘
```

EXERCISE G

Punctuation Practice. Read the sentences and punctuate them. Use periods, commas, and capital letters. Look at the examples.

1. $\overset{M}{m}$y friend's roommate is from $\overset{S}{s}$pain
2. $\overset{H}{h}$e speaks $\overset{S}{s}$panish$_{,}$ $\overset{F}{f}$rench$_{,}$and $\overset{I}{i}$talian
3. his full name is jorge gonzalez
4. he was born in barcelona spain
5. he was born on january 19 1970
6. his address is 1568 main street
7. his family lives in madrid spain
8. his hair is black
9. he is studying english in detroit michigan

86

10. he bought a new car after he came to the u s

11. he wants to get a driver's license because he has a new car

12. he must get a drivers license before he can drive

13. he must also get car insurance before he drives

14. he shouldnt drive his car without insurance

EXERCISE H

Sequence. Read these sentences. They tell how to start a car. They are not in the correct order. Number them in the correct order. Look at the examples.

___ Put the key in the ignition.

_2_ Be sure the car is in neutral or park.

___ Turn the key.

___ Step gently on the gas.

_1_ Open the door, sit down, and close the door.

___ Release the hand brake.

___ Shift to drive.

___ Drive away.

Writing Practice A. Tell how to start a car. Begin with this sentence: "It is easy to start a car." Use these words: first, then, after that, finally.

_____

_____

_____

_____

_____

_____

_____

After you finish writing, discuss the paragraph with your teacher. Your teacher will help you with grammar, vocabulary and organization. Then revise and rewrite your paragraph.

Writing Practice B. Look at the picture below. Tell a story about it. Remember to indent. Here are some words you can use.

kitchen	spatula	frying pan
stove	be careful	

_____

_____

_____

_____

_____

_____

_____

_____

_____

Lesson 13
SPORTS

Soccer Volleyball Football

Tennis Golf Running

1. There are many sports.
   There are team sports.
   There are individual sports.

2. Soccer is a team sport.
   Football is a team sport.
   Volleyball is a team sport.

3. Golf is an individual sport.
   Swimming is an individual sport.
   Running is an individual sport.

4. Soccer is the most popular team sport.

5. There are eleven players on a soccer team.
   The players wear uniforms.
   The players wear shirts, shorts, shoes, and socks.

6. Each team tries to make a goal.
   Each team tries to kick the ball into the other team's goal.
   The players must not touch the ball with their hands.

7. In England, soccer is the same as American football.
   In the United States, there are two different games: football and soccer.

8. Many people think that soccer is better than football because it is safer.

COMPARISONS

Positive	Comparative	Superlative
Adjective	*Compare only two*	*Compare three or more*
good	better	the best
bad	worse	the worst
small	smaller	the smallest
large	larger	the largest
big	bigger	the biggest
fast	faster	the fastest
tall	taller	the tallest
nice	nicer	the nicest
	more	the most
intelligent	more intelligent	the most intelligent
beautiful	more beautiful	the most beautiful
expensive	more expensive	the most expensive
interesting	more interesting	the most interesting
popular	more popular	the most popular

If a word has three or more syllables, use *more* or *most*. Do not add *er* or *est*.

in∗tel∗li∗gent   (4 syllables)

ex∗pen∗sive   (3 syllables)

EXERCISE A

Read the sentences. Fill in each space with the correct word. Look at the examples.

1. Bill was the _tallest_ player on the team.
   taller/tall/tallest

2. Steve was the __*best*__ kicker on the team.
   best/good/better

3. Soccer is the _____ popular team sport in the world.
   more/most

4. Is Steve the _____ player on the team?
   worse/worst/bad

5. Some people think that volleyball is _____ than golf.
   interesting/more interesting/most interesting

6. A football is _____ than a soccer ball.
   long/longer/longest

7. Soccer is _____ than football.
   safer/safe/safest

8. Running is the _____ popular individual sport.
   more/most

9. Running is _____ than walking.
   fast/faster/fastest

10. Pelé was the _____ soccer player in the world.
    best/better/good

11. Running shoes are usually _____ than soccer shoes.
    expensive/more expensive/most expensive

12. This soccer ball is _____ than that one.
    larger/largest/large

13. Some people like tennis _____ than volleyball.
    best/better/good

EXERCISE B

Look at the drawings in Figure 13–1 on page 92. Compare the things that you see. Using the following adjectives, write three sentences about each group.

1. expensive

   _____

   _____

   _____

2. big

   _____

   _____

   _____

3. happy

   _____

   _____

   _____

FIGURE 13-1

AND

And joins two equal ideas. Look at these examples.

Jim likes to play volleyball *and* soccer.
Evelyn *and* Alex want to buy a house.
George needs to buy a large *and* inexpensive car.

Punctuation. When *and* joins two sentences, you must use a comma before it.

The soccer team is very good, *and* it is going to play in the Olympics.

And sometimes joins a series of items. Use *and* only before the last word in a series of three or more.

My brother plays volleyball, soccer, and basketball.
Running, swimming, and bicycling are good exercise.

EXERCISE C

Read the sentences. Then combine them with *and,* using commas wherever they are necessary. Look at the examples.

1. There are team sports.
    There are individual sports.
    <u>There are team sports and individual sports.</u>

2. Soccer is a team sport.
    Football is a team sport.
    Volleyball is a team sport.
    <u>Soccer, football, and volleyball are team sports.</u>

3. Golf is an individual sport.
    Swimming is an individual sport.
    Running is an individual sport.

    _____

    _____

4. Soccer players wear shirts.
    Soccer players wear shorts.
    Soccer players wear shoes.
    Soccer players wear socks.

    _____

    _____

5. Americans like to play soccer.
    Americans like to play football.

    _____

    _____

6. Henry likes to play football.
    Henry likes to play soccer.
    Henry likes to play volleyball.

    _____

    _____

7. Soccer players wear uniforms.
    Volleyball players wear uniforms.

    _____

    _____

8. Running is a popular sport.
    Soccer is a popular sport.
    Football is a popular sport.

    _____

    _____

PRONOUNS

Pronouns take the place of nouns.

the players = they

each team = it

Steve = he

Alice = she

you and I = we

They, it, he, she, we, you, and *I* are pronouns.

EXERCISE D

Pronoun Practice. Read these sentences. The same nouns are found in each pair of sentences. Change the noun in the second sentence to a pronoun. Look at the example.

1. The players wear uniforms.
   The players wear shorts, shirts, shoes, and socks.
   <u>They wear shorts, shirts, shoes, and socks.</u>

2. My friend and I always try to make a goal.
   My friend and I try to kick the ball into the other team's goal.

3. Steve is a good kicker.
   Steve is the best kicker on the team.

4. Henry can run faster than Steve.
   Henry is the fastest runner on the team.

5. Hana likes to play soccer.
   Hana plays soccer very well.

6. Running is an individual sport.
   Running is very popular.

7. Many people think soccer is better than football.
   Soccer is safer.

   _____

   _____

8. Players must not touch the ball with their hands.
   The players must kick the ball.

   _____

   _____

EXERCISE E

Read the sentences and combine them, using *and* or *because.* With *and,* use a comma. Instead of repeating a noun, use a pronoun. Look at the examples.

1. Football players sometimes hurt their heads.
   Football players wear helmets.
   <u>Football players wear helmets because they</u>
   <u>sometimes hurt their heads.</u>

2. It snows in the winter time.
   Many people like to ski and skate.
   <u>It snows in the winter time, and many</u>
   <u>people like to ski and skate.</u>

3. Many people like to play volleyball.
   People can play volleyball almost anywhere.

   _____

   _____

4. Running is good exercise.
   Many people run several miles every day.

   _____

   _____

5. Soccer players can run easily.
   Soccer players wear shoes with cleats.

   _____

   _____

6. There are eleven players on a soccer team.
   There are eleven players on a football team.

   _____

   _____

7. Soccer players must kick the ball. Soccer players cannot touch the soccer ball
   with their hands.

   _____

   _____

8. In England, the most popular game is soccer.
   In the U.S., the most popular game is football.

   _____

   _____

9. Soccer is safer than football.
   Many people think soccer is better than football.

   _____

   _____

10. Volleyball players must hit the ball up in the air.
    The ball must go over the net.

    _____

    _____

11. Volleyball is a team sport.
    Swimming is an individual sport.

    _____

    _____

12. Argentina won the World Cup in 1978.
    Italy won the World Cup in 1982.

    _____

    _____

Dictation. With your teacher and classmates, write a paragraph about sports. Your teacher will dictate something similar.

_____

_____

_____

_____

Writing Practice A. Look at each picture and the vocabulary words. Write four or five sentences about each picture. Use complete sentences.

1. tennis player
   tennis racket
   tennis ball
   Mark

_____

_____

_____

_____

2. basketball player
   basketball court
   basketball
   shorts and jersey

_____

_____

_____

_____

3. baseball
   cap
   glove
   throw
   Manuel

_____

_____

_____

_____

_____

4. swimming
   pool
   swimmer
   fastest
   lane
   goggles

_____

_____

_____

_____

Writing Practice B. Write about your favorite sport. Begin with this sentence:
_____ is my favorite sport because _____ .

For example: (Soccer) is my favorite sport because (I can play anywhere.)
(Swimming) is my favorite sport because (it is an individual sport.)

_____

_____

_____

_____

_____

_____

_____

_____

Discuss the paragraph and possible revisions with your teacher. Then revise and rewrite it.

Lesson 14
THE OLYMPICS

1. The Olympic Games began in ancient Greece.
   They honored the Greek god Zeus.
   Zeus was the king of the gods.

2. The best person in each event won the game.
   He was the winner.
   There were no stopwatches then.
   The best man won.

3. The modern Olympics occur every four years.
   There are Olympic Games in the summer and in the winter.
   Athletes compete in individual and team events.

4. Two individual events from the winter Olympic Games are ice-skating and skiing.
   Two team events from the summer Olympic Games are the 400-meter relay race and volleyball.

5. Amateur athletes work hard before the Olympic Games.
   They train for many months with a coach.
   They want to win a medal for their country.
   They don't want to lose.

6. The first-place winner wins a gold medal.
   The second-place winner wins a silver medal.
   The third-place winner wins a bronze medal.

7. Most athletes know only their teammates when the Olympic Games begin.
   The athletes have friends from many countries when the Games end.
   Athletes win medals and friends.

8. The Olympics are important for athletes and for world peace and friendship.

COMMANDS

Commands tell people to do something.

Run faster!	Don't jump the gun.
Jump higher!	Don't be late for practice.
Be a good sport.	Don't be a bad sport.

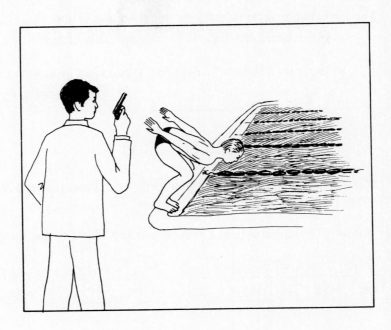

EXERCISE A

Choose a sport, and imagine that you are a coach. Tell your athletes what to do and what not to do. Use commands.

in the morning

_____

_____

in the afternoon

_____

_____

at night

_____

_____

BUT and SO

But shows contrast or differences.

> The soccer player wants to win, but he doesn't want to practice.
> The team members played a good game, but they lost.
> They practiced hard but lost.

So shows result.

> The gymnast practiced hard, so she won a gold medal.
> The bicyclist broke his leg, so he was not able to ride.

Punctuation.   Use a comma before *but* and *so* when they join two complete sentences.

EXERCISE B

Read the sentences. Combine them to make one sentence, using *but* or *so*. Look at the examples.

1. The 1984 Summer Olympics were in Los Angeles. The 1988 Olympics will be in Seoul, Korea.

   The 1984 Summer Olympics were in Los Angeles, but the 1988 Olympics will be in Seoul, Korea.

2. Ice-skating and ice hockey are winter sports. These events are in the Winter Olympics.

Ice-skating and ice hockey are winter sports, so these events are in the Winter Olympics.

3. A soccer field is eighty yards wide. A football field is fifty-three yards wide.

_____

_____

4. A football is oval. A soccer ball is round.

_____

_____

5. Soccer players cannot touch the ball with their hands. They must kick the ball.

_____

_____

6. Football players can tackle other players. Football is a dangerous game.

_____

_____

7. A soccer match is ninety minutes long. A football game is sixty minutes long.

_____

_____

8. That man played soccer for money. He cannot compete in the Olympics.

_____

_____

9. Athletes train for many years. They can compete in the Olympics.

_____

_____

10. Everyone wants to win. All players try to do their best.

_____

_____

Dictation. With your teacher and classmates, write a paragraph about the Olympics. Your teacher will dictate something similar.

_____

_____

_____

_____

_____

_____

EXERCISE C

Punctuation. Read the sentences and punctuate them. Use commas, capital letters, periods, and apostrophes.

1. thousands of runners carry the olympic torch from olympic greece to the host country
2. nadia comaneci was a gymnast from romania
3. a decathlon athlete is in ten events
4. bruce jenner won a gold medal for the united states in the decathlon in 1976 in montreal
5. athletes play water polo in a swimming pool
6. men and women do not compete together in basketball cycling swimming and diving events
7. women do not compete in boxing or soccer
8. there is a womens volleyball team and a mens volleyball team

9. the closing ceremony of the olympics is after the last event

10. an athlete puts out the olympic torch

11. all the athletes go to their countries

EXERCISE D

Pronouns. Read the paragraph. Fill in each space with a pronoun. Look at the example.

Every four years the Olympic Games are in a different country. The host countries need to plan carefully for _them_ . _____ sometimes plan for many years before the games begin. _____ must be able to feed thousands of athletes three meals a day for several weeks. _____ must also find housing for the athletes and visitors.

The Olympic Games begin with an opening ceremony. _____ is usually a very big show. The leader of the country opens the games. _____ makes a speech and there is a big parade with all of the athletes. _____ march with their teammates and carry the flag of their country. _____ sometimes wear the traditional dress of their country. The athletes from Greece come first, and they carry the Greek flag. _____ is blue and white. After the opening ceremony, the games begin. _____ last for two or three weeks. The winners of each event win medals. _____ are very happy.

Writing Practice A. Read about these situations, and use your imagination.

1. Imagine that you are an ex-student from this school. Tell a new student what to do and what not to do at school. Use commands.

   _____

   _____

   _____

   _____

2. Tell a new student from your country what to do and what not to do in the United States. Use commands.

   _____

   _____

   _____

   _____

Writing Practice B. Look at the picture above, and write a story about it. Remember to indent. Here are some words you can use.

kick   field   uniform   team
watch   practice   picnic

_____

_____

_____

_____

_____

_____

_____

_____

_____

_____

Lesson 15

GEOGRAPHY OF THE UNITED STATES

1. The United States is in North America.
   The capital is Washington, D.C.
   Washington is on the East Coast, near the Atlantic Ocean.

2. There are fifty states in the United States.
   Alaska and Hawaii are the newest states.
   Hawaii is a group of islands in the Pacific Ocean.
   Alaska is the largest state.
   Rhode Island is the smallest state.

3. The population of the United States is more than 200 million.
   People from many countries live in the United States.

4. The Mississippi River is the longest river in the United States.
   The Rocky Mountains are the highest mountains.
   The Rocky Mountains are in the West.
   The five Great Lakes are in the Northeast.
   The Mojave desert is in the Southwest.

5. The weather is very cold in the North.
   There is a lot of snow in the winter.
   The weather is hot in the South.
   It is warm and pleasant in the winter.

6. Mexico is south of the United States.
   Canada is north of the United States.
   The Atlantic Ocean is east of the United States.
   The Pacific Ocean is west of the United States.

7. The United States has many natural resources.
   There is good land for agriculture.
   There is petroleum for fuel.
   There is water.
   There is much industry.

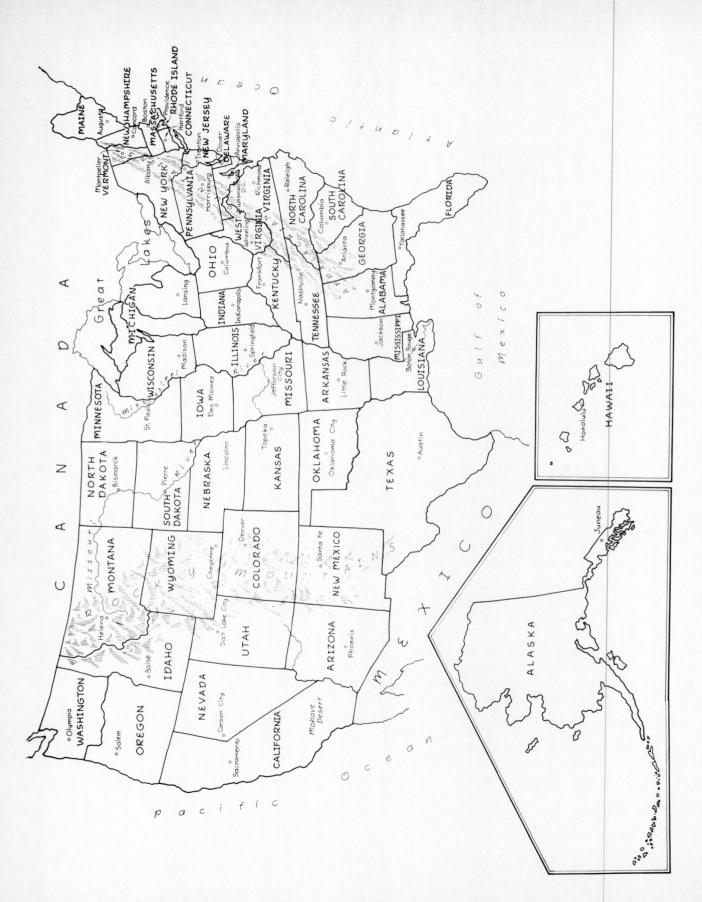

Dictation. With your teacher and classmates, write a paragraph about the United States. Your teacher will dictate something similar.

_____

_____

_____

_____

Punctuation. Capitalize the names of geographic places: rivers, mountains, lakes, cities.

the Colorado River	the Rocky Mountains
Lake Erie	San Francisco

EXERCISE A

Punctuation Practice. Read these sentences, and then punctuate them. Use commas, capital letters, and periods. Look at the example.

1. california is on the west coast of the united states
2. the pacific ocean is west of california
3. the state of oregon is north of california and mexico is south of california
4. sacramento is the capital of california
5. the largest cities are san francisco los angeles and san diego

EXERCISE B

Pronoun Practice. Read the sentences. When you find a noun in both sentences, change the one in the second sentence to a pronoun. Look at the example.

1. The United States is a large country.
   The United States is in North America.
   The United States is a large country. It is in
   North America.

2. The capital is Washington, D.C.
   Washington, D.C. is on the East Coast.

   _____

   _____

3. There are more than 200 million people in the United States.
   The people come from many different countries.

   _____

   _____

4. The Mississippi River is the longest river in the United States.
The Mississippi River divides the country in half.

_____

_____

5. The Rocky Mountains are the highest mountains.
The Rocky Mountains are in the West.

_____

_____

6. There are five Great Lakes.
The Great Lakes are in the Northeast.

_____

_____

7. The Mojave Desert is in the Southwest.
The Mojave Desert is the hottest part of the U.S.

_____

_____

EXERCISE C

Read the groups of words. Then write sentences about them, using the superlative.
Use *the most* or *est.* Look at the examples.

1. the Himalayan Mountains/high/world

   The Himalayan Mountains are the highest in the world.

2. New York/expensive/city/United States

   New York is the most expensive city in the United States.

3. the Sahara Desert/large/world

   _____

4. the Nile River/long/Africa

   _____

5. the Rocky Mountains/high/United States

   _____

6. Los Angeles/polluted/city/California

   _____

7. the Mississippi River/long/North America

   _____

8. Greenland/large/island/world

   _____

9. the Pacific Ocean/large/world

   _____

10. Mexico City/interesting/city/North America

_____

11. the Amazon River/dangerous/South America

_____

12. Mt. Everest/cold/mountain/world

_____

EXERCISE D

Look at the map of North America above and read the sentences. They are not true. Change the italicized word to make the sentence true. Look at the example.

1. Mexico is *north* of the United States.
   Mexico is south of the United States.

2. The capital of Mexico is *Guadalajara.*

_____

3. The Gulf of Mexico is *west* of Mexico.

_____

4. Lower California is part of *the United States*.

_____

5. The United States is *south* of Mexico.

_____

6. Canada is north of *Mexico*.

_____

7. *Toronto* is the capital of Canada.

_____

8. The five Great Lakes are in *Canada*.

_____

9. *New York City* is the capital of the United States.

_____

THE

In general, do not use *the* with names of people, sports, meals, or places.

Los Angeles	Mt. Everest
California	Lake Michigan
Mexico	Maui
Cairo	football
volleyball	Mr. Smith
John Wilson	breakfast

John Wilson and Mrs. Smith ate breakfast after they played volleyball on Maui.

But you must use *the* with some names.

1. groups of mountains   the Rocky Mountains
   groups of lakes   the Great Lakes
   groups of islands   the Hawaiian Islands
   countries with   the United States
   United or *Republic* in their names   the Republic of China

2. oceans, seas, and rivers   the Pacific Ocean
       the Red Sea
       the Gulf of Mexico
       the Nile River
       the Bay of Bengal
       the Mississippi River

3. deserts   the Sahara Desert

4. only one country uses *the*   the Sudan

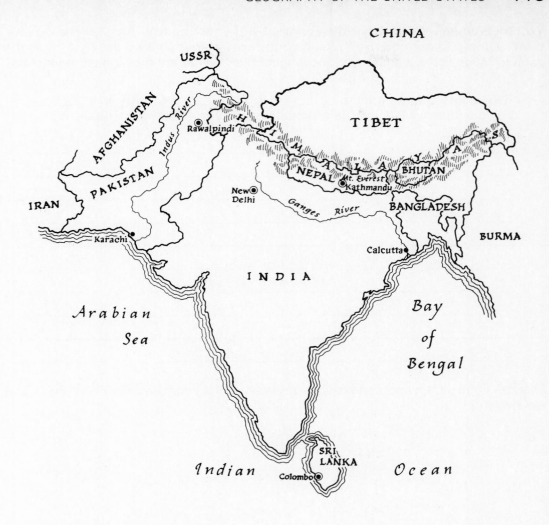

EXERCISE E

Read the paragraph. Fill in the blanks with *the* only if necessary.

_____ India is a large country in southern _____ Asia. The capital of _____ India is _____ New Delhi. The official languages are _____ English and _____ Hindi. The longest river is _____ Ganges River. _____ Tibet, _____ Nepal, and _____ Bhutan are north of _____ India. _____ Pakistan is west, and _____ Bangladesh is east. _____ India is a peninsula with _____ Arabian Sea to the southwest and _____ Bay of Bengal to the east. _____ Himalayan Mountains and _____ Mt. Everest border _____ India to the north.

Writing Practice. Write about the geography of your country. Answer these questions. Where is your country? Which countries are near your country? What is the capital? What is the biggest city, the longest river? What are the highest mountains?

Begin with this sentence: _____ is a _____ country in _____ .
For example: (Malaysia) is a (small) country in (Southeast Asia).

_____

_____

_____

_____

_____

_____

_____

_____

_____

Discuss your paragraph and possible revisions with your teacher. Then revise and rewrite it.

Lesson 16
DESERTS

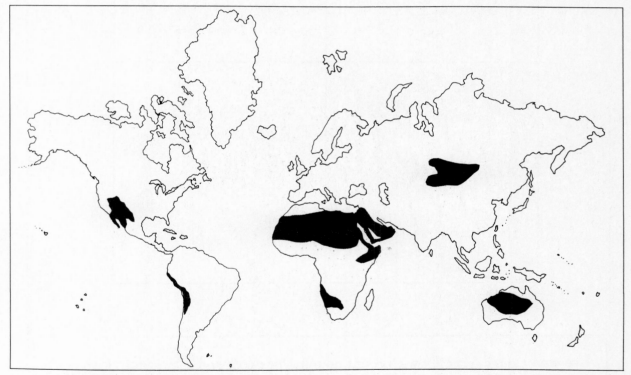

1. Deserts are hot and dry.
   One seventh (1/7) of the earth is desert.

2. Sand covers 10–20% of the deserts.
   Sand dunes are sand mountains.
   Some sand dunes are 820 feet (250 meters) high.

3. There is only a little rain in the desert.
   Not much can live in the desert without water.
   Not many people live in deserts.

4. Some people live in oases in deserts.
   There is a lot of water underground in an oasis.
   Palm trees grow in oases.
   Dates grow on palm trees.

5. Other people live in the desert.
They have animals.
They move from place to place.
They are looking for water.

Use *many* and *a few* only with count nouns. Use *much* and *a little* only with non-count nouns. Use *some, no,* and *a lot of* with either count or noncount nouns. Pay attention to *much, many, a little,* and *a few.*

Count nouns	Noncount nouns
many people	much water
not many people	not much water
a few people	a little rain
a few animals	a little sand
no people	no rain
no trees	no snow

EXERCISE A

Read the sentences. They are not true. Change the italicized word to make these false statements true. Look at the examples.

1. *Many* people live in the desert.
   Not many people live in the desert.

2. There is *no* rain in the desert.
   There is only a little rain in the desert.

3. *Many* people live in oases.

   _____

4. There is *a little* underground water in an oasis.

   _____

5. There are *a few* palm trees in an oasis.

   _____

6. *Few* dates grow on palm trees.

   _____

7. *Many* plants grow in deserts.

   _____

8. *Many* people live in deserts.

   _____

9. There is *a lot of* water in deserts.

   _____

10. Nepal has *a few* mountains.

   _____

NOUN PLURALS

Some noun plurals are irregular. Study these.

| oasis | oases | sheep | sheep | person | people |

Some nouns add *es* to form the plural.

| bush | bushes | grass | grasses |

EXERCISE B

Read the sentences, and then fill in each blank with the correct singular or plural form of the noun in parentheses. Look at the examples.

1. Desert people often have __sheep__ . (sheep)
2. There are many palm trees in an __oasis__ . (oasis)
3. There are usually _____ and _____ near a river. (tree, bush)
4. _____ are the center of life in the desert. (oasis)
5. There are five major _____ in the world. (desert)
6. The _____ are playing with a _____ . (child, sheep)

EXERCISE C

Read the sentences, and then fill in each blank with *much, many, a few,* or *a little.* Look at the examples.

1. There are _a few_ deserts in the world.
2. There is _much_ sand in deserts.
3. There are _____ sand dunes in deserts.
4. There is _____ rain in deserts.
5. There are _____ people in deserts.
6. There are _____ oases in deserts.
7. There are _____ palm trees in oases.
8. _____ dates grow on palm trees.
9. There are _____ plants in deserts.
10. There is _____ sand in deserts.
11. _____ people live in deserts.
12. Oases have _____ palm trees.
13. Palm trees have _____ dates.
14. Desert plants need only _____ water.

EXERCISE D

Read the groups of words, and then write sentences with them. Be sure to punctuate them correctly. Look at the examples.

1. palm trees/desert

   There are many palm trees in the desert.

2. people/live/desert

   Not many people live in the desert.

3. the Mojave Desert/the United States

_____

4. it/hot/desert

_____

5. some people/have/sheep/desert

_____

6. sheep/goats/camels/desert animals

_____

7. the mesquite tree/find/water/because/it/have/long roots

_____

_____

8. there/water/oasis

_____

9. some plants/fat/after/it/rain

_____

10. camels/need/water

_____

FRACTIONAL FIGURES

Fractional figures can be written two ways. You may write them as fractions or percents. For example, 1/2 can be written either *one half* or *fifty percent*. Fractions such as 1/7 or 1/3 are often written out. Except for one half, fractions use cardinal numbers in the numerator and ordinal numbers in the denominator. Study these examples.

1/5 = one fifth	3/5 = three fifths
1/8 = one eighth	5/8 = five eighths
1/16 = one sixteenth	7/16 = seven sixteenths

Except for *first*, *second*, and *third*, ordinal numbers are formed by adding *th* to the cardinal number. Notice these irregular spellings: fi*f*th, ni*n*th, twel*f*th.

EXERCISE E

Write each of these fractions two ways. Use both fractions and percents. Look at the example.

1. 1/3   one third   thirty-three percent
2. 2/3 _____ _____
3. 3/4 _____ _____

4. 1/5 _____   _____
5. 1/2 _____   _____
6. 1/8 _____   _____
7. 3/10 _____   _____
8. 1/20 _____   _____

SO and BECAUSE

So and *because* both show cause and result. Look at the examples.

People use camels in the desert *because* they can store water for a long time.
Camels can store water for a long time, *so* people use them in the desert.

EXERCISE F

Read these sentences. Then combine them with *because* or *so*. Look at the example.

1. Not many plants can live in the desert.
   There is little water.   (so)

   There is little water, so not many plants can live
   in the desert.

2. An oasis has many palm trees.
   There is water underground.   (because)

   _____

   _____

3. Their animals need water.
   Desert people move from place to place.   (because)

   _____

   _____

4. There are few plants in the desert.
   Plants need water.   (so)

   _____

   _____

5. Some desert plants have very long roots.
   They can find water underground.   (so)

   _____

   _____

6. Some desert plants do not lose water.
   They do not have leaves.   (because)

   _____

   _____

7. Other desert plants hold water in their stems.
   They can use the water in dry weather.   (so)

_____

_____

EXERCISE G

Pronoun Practice. Read these sentences. Some nouns are repeated in the second sentence. Change the nouns in the second sentence to pronouns. Look at the example.

1. Deserts are hot and dry.
   Deserts cover one seventh of the earth.

   Deserts are hot and dry. They cover one seventh
   of the earth.

2. Sand dunes are sand mountains.
   Sand dunes sometimes move across the desert.

   _____

   _____

3. There is only a little rain in the desert.
   All plants and animals need rain to live.

   _____

   _____

4. Some people live in the desert.
   These people move from place to place.

   _____

   _____

5. Palm trees grow in oases.
   Many dates grow on palm trees.

   _____

   _____

6. Some plants can live in the desert.
   Some plants can get water.

   _____

   _____

7. This plant has sharp thorns.
   The thorns protect the plant from animals.
   Animals want to eat the plant.

   _____

   _____

8. Water is necessary in the desert.
   Plants and animals cannot live without water.

_____

_____

Dictation. With your teacher and classmates, write a paragraph about the desert. Your teacher will dictate something similar.

_____

_____

_____

_____

Punctuation.   Capitalize the names of geographical locations, such as deserts, seas, oceans, and countries.

   the Sahara Desert   the Atlantic Ocean

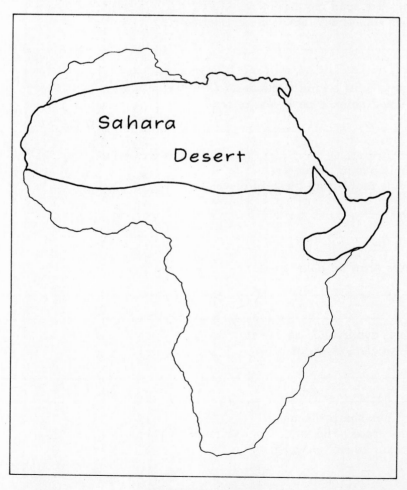

The Sahara Desert

EXERCISE H

Punctuation. Read these sentences and punctuate them. Use capital letters, commas, and periods. Look at the example.

1. The Sahara Desert is the largest desert in the world
2. it is in north africa
3. it covers three and a half million square miles
4. three and a half million square miles is the same as nine million square kilometers
5. the sahara desert goes from the red sea to the atlantic ocean
6. it covers parts of morocco algeria tunisia libya sudan chad niger mali and mauritania
7. the word *sahara* comes from the arabic word *sahra'*
8. *sahra'* means *desert* in arabic

Writing Practice A. Write several sentences about your hometown. Tell where it is and describe its geography. Begin with '' _____ is my hometown.''

_____

_____

_____

_____

_____

_____

_____

Discuss the paragraph and possible revisions with your teacher. Then revise and rewrite it.

Navajo family in northern Arizona

Writing Practice B. Look at the picture above. Write a story about it. Here are some words you can use.

Navajo   Indians   herd of sheep
horse   grass

_____

_____

_____

_____

_____

_____

_____

_____

_____

_____

_____

_____

Lesson 17
LIFE IN THE PAST

1. One hundred years ago, there were no cars.
   People rode horses.
   They drove wagons.

2. There were no supermarkets.
   Families raised animals for meat.
   They grew their own vegetables.

3. There was no television.
   People sat around the fire at night.
   They talked.
   They told stories.
   They played games.

4. There were no electric lights.
   People used candles.
   They went to bed early.

5. There were no electric machines.
   Women worked hard at home.
   They cooked on wood stoves.
   They baked their own bread.
   They made the clothes for their families.

PAST TENSE
Add *ed* to form the past tense of regular verbs.

cook	cooked
watch	watched
talk	talked
play	played

If the verb ends in *e*, add only *d*.

bake	baked
use	used
raise	raised

If the verb ends in a *y* preceded by a consonant, change the *y* to *i* and add *ed*.

dry	dried
study	studied

Many verbs are irregular. Study these irregular past-tense forms.

ride	rode	tell	told
drive	drove	read	read
write	wrote	hurt	hurt
sit	sat	grow	grew
am	was	make	made
are	were	do	did
is	was	go	went
have	had	sing	sang
buy	bought	teach	taught

EXERCISE A

Read the sentences and fill in each blank with the past tense of the verbs in parentheses. Look at the examples.

1. Life in the past __was__ different from today. (be)

2. People __rode__ horses, or they __walked__ to work. (ride, walk)

3. There _____ no televisions, so people _____ at night. (be, talk)

4. They _____ the newspaper by candlelight. (read)

5. Many people _____ on farms because there _____ few cities. (live, be)

6. There _____ no electricity, so people _____ with wood. (be, cook)

7. People _____ animals for meat. (raise)

8. People _____ vegetables in their gardens because there _____ no supermarkets. (grow, be)

9. There _____ not many schools, so many children _____ to study at home. (be, have)

10. Women _____ clothes for their families. (make)

11. People sometimes _____ letters because there _____ no telephones. (write, be)

12. They _____ only a few things at the general store. (buy)

EXERCISE B

Read the sentence and fill in each blank with either the simple present or the simple past. Look at the examples.

1. There __are__ fifty states in the United States. (be)

2. Everyone __did__ the homework last night. (do)

3. Harry _____ to the movie almost every weekend. (go)

4. People _____ very hard in the past. (work)

5. People _____ very hard now too. (work)

6. Five students _____ in the front row. (sit)

7. My mother _____ cookies every week. (bake)

8. The student _____ a letter to his family last Saturday. (write)

9. When he was a child, his family _____ on a farm. (live)

10. There _____ always a lot of homework. (be)

EXERCISE C

Read this paragraph about life in the past. Fill in the blank with the past form of a verb. Some spaces may have more than one correct answer. Look at the examples.

One hundred and fifty years ago, there _were_ no machines. There _were_ no cars, and there _____ no electricity. People did not _____ cars, so they _____ horses. People did not _____ bread in the supermarket. They _____ bread at home. They did not _____ television at night. They _____ around the fire and _____ . They did not _____ electric lights, so they _____ letters and books by candlelight. They did not _____ telephones, so they _____ letters. Life was different from today.

Dictation. With your teacher and classmates, write a paragraph about life in the past. Your teacher will dictate something similar.

_____

_____

_____

_____

_____

_____

AND and OR

You may join words in a series with *and*.

I want apples. I want bananas. I want oranges.
I want apples, bananas, and oranges.

In a negative series, use *or*.

I don't eat fish. I don't eat pork. I don't eat cake.
I don't eat fish, pork, or cake.

128

EXERCISE D

Read the sentences and combine them with *and* or *or* to make one sentence. Look at the example.

1. One hundred years ago, there were no supermarkets.
   There were no drugstores.
   There were no shopping malls.

   One hundred years ago, there were no supermarkets,
   drugstores, or shopping malls.

2. People bought soap at the general store.
   People bought spices at the general store.
   People bought tools at the general store.
   People bought material at the general store.
   People bought food at the general store.

   _____

   _____

3. They talked to their friends there.
   They talked to their relatives there.
   They talked to their neighbors there.

   _____

   _____

4. The general store did not have ice cream.
   They general store did not have toothpaste.
   The general store did not have toasters.

   _____

   _____

5. People did not have radios.
   People did not have television.
   People did not have electric lights.

   _____

   _____

6. In the evening, people sometimes visited friends.
   People sat around the fire.
   People told stories.
   People often sang songs.

   _____

   _____

7. On farms, people raised cows for milk.
   People raised chickens for eggs.
   People raised sheep for meat.

   _____

   _____

EXERCISE E

Sentence Practice. Review *before* and *after*. Write four sentences with *before*. Look at the example.

1. *There were no electric lights before Thomas Edison invented the light bulb.*
2. *People wrote letters before* _____
   _____
3. _____
   _____
4. _____
   _____
5. _____
   _____

Write four sentences with *after*. Look at the example.

1. *Many children watch television after they come home from school.*
2. *Students* _____
   _____
3. _____
   _____
4. _____
   _____
5. _____
   _____

Writing Practice A. Write some sentences about life in the past in your hometown. Explain what your grandparents did.

_____
_____
_____
_____
_____
_____

Writing Practice B. Tell about life in your hometown today, and what you do when you are there.

_____

_____

_____

_____

_____

_____

_____

_____

_____

_____

_____

Discuss your paragraphs and possible revisions with your teacher. Then revise and rewrite them.

Lesson 18
BIOGRAPHY

Mahatma Ghandi   Martin Luther King, Jr.   Malcolm X

1. Martin Luther King, Jr. was a leader of the black people in North America.
   He helped black Americans win equality.

2. He was born in Georgia on January 15, 1929.
   He grew up in Atlanta, Georgia.
   His father was a Baptist minister.

3. He went to Morehouse College in Atlanta.
   He received his B.A. degree in 1948.

4. He wanted to be a doctor or a lawyer.
   He decided to become a minister.

5. He studied to become a minister.
   He learned about Mahatma Gandhi.
   He became minister of a Baptist church in Montgomery, Alabama.
   He received his Ph.D. degree.

6. He met Coretta Scott in Boston.
   They were married in 1953.
   They had four children.

7. He led the March on Washington in 1963.
   Two hundred thousand people came to Washington, D.C.
   They wanted equality for all people, black and white.
   Dr. King said, "I have a dream . . ."

8. James Earl Ray killed Dr. King on April 4, 1968 in Memphis, Tennessee.

PUNCTUATION

Use a comma between the names of cities and states.

Montgomery, Alabama

Use capital letters for the names of

religions	Baptist
colleges	Morehouse
titles	Dr. King
degrees	Ph.D.

Use a period after a title.   Dr. King

EXERCISE A

Punctuation Practice. Read the sentences and punctuate them. Use periods, commas, and capital letters. Look at the example.

1. ~~m~~alcolm ~~x~~ was also a leader of ~~a~~merican blacks
2. his name was malcolm little
3. he was born on may 19 1925 in omaha nebraska
4. his father was also a baptist minister
5. he went to prison when he was twenty-one
6. he became a black muslim in prison
7. he became a black muslim minister in new york
8. he was a militant black leader
9. malcolm believed in violence to get freedom
10. he made a pilgrimage to mecca in 1964
11. his autobiography teaches many important lessons
12. he was killed in harlem new york on february 21 1965

PREPOSITIONS

Use *in* and *on* with dates. Use *in* with the month or year: *in* January; *in* 1925.
    Use *on* with the day: *on* January 15, 1929.

Use *in* with cities and states. He lived *in* Boston.

To shows direction. They walked *to* Washington, D.C.

EXERCISE B

Read the sentence and fill in each blank with the preposition *in, on,* or *to.* Look at the examples.

1. Joseph P. Kennedy was born __on__ September 6, 1888 __in__ Boston, Massachusetts.

2. He went _____ Great Britain _____ 1937 as the United States ambassador.

3. His wife, Rose Fitzgerald, was born _____ Boston _____ July 22, 1890.

4. Joseph Kennedy died _____ Hyannisport, Massachusetts _____ November, 1969.

5. John F. Kennedy was their son. He was born _____ Brookline, Massachusetts _____ May 29, 1917.

6. He went _____ Congress _____ 1947.

7. He became President of the United States _____ 1960.

8. He was killed _____ Dallas, Texas _____ November, 1963.

134

EXERCISE C

Read the sentences. Then combine them, using *before, after,* or *when.* Look at the examples.

1. Martin Luther King went to Morehouse College.
   He was fifteen years old.

   Martin Luther King went to Morehouse College when he was fifteen years old.

2. The buses were segregated.
   Dr. King protested.

   The buses were segregated before Dr. King protested.

3. He wanted to be a doctor.
   He became a minister.

   _____

   _____

4. He studied about Mahatma Gandhi.
   He was in school.

   _____

   _____

5. Black and white people were not equal.
   The Civil Rights Act became law.

   _____

   _____

6. Malcolm Little was a Baptist.
   He went to prison.

   _____

   _____

7. He became a Black Muslim.
   He was in prison.

   _____

   _____

8. Malcolm X made the pilgrimage to Mecca.
   He learned about true Islam.

   _____

   _____

9. He believed in violence.
   He went to Mecca.

   _____

   _____

10. His thinking changed.
    He went to Mecca.

    _____

    _____

11. He began to work with Dr. King.
    He was killed.

    _____

    _____

12. Malcolm X and Dr. King were both killed.
    They worked for civil rights.

    _____

    _____

AND and BUT

And joins ideas that show similarity. *And* also gives additional information. *But* shows differences and contrast.

EXERCISE D

Dr. King and Malcolm X had the same goal: equality for their people. They used very different ways to get this goal. Read the sentences and combine them with *but* or *and.* Look at the examples.

1. Martin Luther King graduated from college.
   Malcolm X did not go to college.

   Martin Luther King graduated from college, but Malcolm X did not go to college.

2. Martin Luther King grew up in the South.
   Malcolm Little grew up in the North.

   Martin Luther King grew up in the South, but Malcolm Little grew up in the North.

3. Martin Luther King had a quiet, peaceful childhood.
   Malcolm Little had a difficult, violent childhood.

   _____

   _____

4. Dr. King believed in nonviolent resistance.
   Malcolm X believed in violent resistance.

   _____

   _____

5. Dr. King attended the University of Boston.
   He received his Ph.D. degree in 1955.

   _____

   _____

6. Malcolm X was a very good speaker.
   Many people listened to him.

   _____

   _____

7. Malcolm X was a Black Muslim minister.
   Dr. King was a Baptist minister.

   _____

   _____

8. Malcolm X left the Black Muslims.
   He started his own religious group.

   _____

   _____

Dictation. With your teacher and classmates, write a paragraph of three or four sentences about the life of Martin Luther King or Malcolm X. Use *before, after,* or *when.* Your teacher will dictate something similar.

_____

_____

_____

_____

_____

EXERCISE E

Read these words and phrases and make complete sentences with them. Use the past form of the verb. Use capital letters, commas, and periods. Look at the example.

1. dr king/civil rights leader

   Dr. King was a civil rights leader.

2. he/born/georgia

   _____

3. malcolm x/another/leader

   _____

4. dr king/go/morehouse college

   _____

5. malcolm x/not go/college

_____

6. dr king/become/baptist minister

_____

7. malcolm x/become/leader/muslim

_____

8. both men/want/equality

_____

9. dr king/believe/nonviolence

_____

10. malcolm x/believe/violence

_____

EXERCISE F

Look at the present form of these regular verbs. Then write the past form. Remember: When the verb ends with _e_, add only _d_. When the verb ends in a _y_ preceded by a consonant, change the _y_ to _i_ and add _ed_.

talk	_____	play	_____	want	_____
kill	_____	work	_____	cook	_____
walk	_____	help	_____	learn	_____
use	_____	bake	_____	dry	_____
raise	_____	decide	_____	study	_____
receive	_____				

Look at the present form of these irregular verbs. Then write the past form.

ride	_____	drive	_____	write	_____
make	_____	read	_____	do	_____
have	_____	begin	_____	go	_____
grow	_____	teach	_____	sit	_____
buy	_____	become	_____	sing	_____
lead	_____	meet	_____	eat	_____
tell	_____	take	_____	sit	_____
are	_____	am	_____	is	_____

Writing Practice A. Write ten sentences with some of the irregular verbs you know. Use the past tense.

1. _____

2. _____

3. _____

4. _____

5. _____

6. _____

7. _____

8. _____

9. _____

10. _____

Writing Practice B. Write several sentences about your own life. Use *before, after, when, because,* and *so.* You may use some of these phrases.

was born	grew up	went to school	lived in
graduated from	moved to	worked	was married

Begin with these sentences:

My name is _____ . I am from _____ , (and/but) I was born in _____ .

_____

_____

_____

_____

_____

_____

_____

_____

_____

Discuss the paragraph and possible revisions with your teacher. Then revise and rewrite it.

Lesson 19
CAMPING

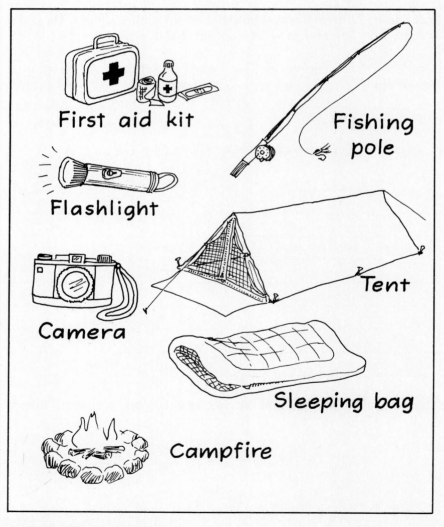

First aid kit

Fishing pole

Flashlight

Camera

Tent

Sleeping bag

Campfire

1. Many people like to go camping.
   Some families travel far to a national park.
   Some families stay close to the city.

2. Bill and his friends are going to go camping next weekend.
   They are going to go to a campground in the mountains.

3. They are going to take many things.
   They will put up a tent at the campsite.
   The campers will sleep in sleeping bags.
   They will put the sleeping bags inside the tent.

4. They are going to bring a flashlight.
   They are going to bring hiking boots.

5. Bill and his friends are going to bring fishing poles because they want to go fishing.

6. Some campers bring binoculars because they want to watch birds.
   Some campers bring a camera because they want to take pictures.

7. Campers often cook their food outdoors.
   Some campers cook their food on a portable stove.
   Bill and his friends are going to cook their food over a campfire.

8. They are going to take matches to start the fire.
   They are going to take pots, pans, dishes, and food.
   They will bring the food in a small ice chest.

9. Campers also bring a first-aid kit.
   They must be prepared for many things.

10. Bill and his friends are going to have a good time.

THE FUTURE

to be + *going to* + *verb* shows the future.

I am going to eat lunch at 12:30 tomorrow.

We can use *will* + *verb* to indicate the future also.

My friends will watch TV at 7:30 tonight.

EXERCISE A

Read the groups of words. Then write a sentence with them, using the future tense.

1. bill/go/camping/next weekend

   Bill will go camping next weekend.

2. he/take/tent

   _____

3. children/watch/birds

   _____

4. they/take/binoculars

   _____

5. parents/bring/food/ice chest

_____

6. family/put up/tent

_____

7. family/sleep/sleeping bags

_____

8. sister/take/camera

_____

QUESTIONS AND NEGATIVE WITH THE FUTURE TENSE

When you use _going to_ for the future, the questions and the negative are the same as with the verb _to be._

    Are you _going to walk_ to the mountains?
    I _am not going to walk_ to the mountains.

When you use _will,_ put it at the beginning of the sentence to make a question. The negative of _will_ is _will not_ or _won't._

    Will he _take_ a camera?
    He _won't take_ a camera.

EXERCISE B

Read the sentences. Then fill in the blanks, making each one negative or a question. Look at the example.

1. Bill and his friends are __not__ going to go camping.

2. His sister is _____ going to bring a camera.

3. _____ they going to cook hamburgers?

4. _____ you put up the tent at noon?

5. _____ they going to go fishing?

6. _____ Bill going to take matches?

7. The campers are _____ going to sleep on beds.

8. _____ you going to bring the flashlight?

9. _____ the family going to drive to the national park?

10. I am _____ going to bring a portable stove.

Dictation. With your teacher and classmates, write a paragraph about camping. Your teacher will dictate something similar.

_____

_____

_____

_____

_____

IF

If is a conditional word. It shows uncertainty. When we are not sure, we use *if*. Look at these examples, paying careful attention to the verbs.

   We are going camping next weekend.

   If it rains, we will sleep in the car.

   If it rains, we can't have a fire.

   If we don't have a fire, we will use the portable stove.

Punctuation.   When *if* begins a sentence, use a comma in the middle.

EXERCISE C

Read the phrases. Then finish them, making complete sentences. Use *if*. Look at the example.

1. If Bill takes a camera, _he can take pictures_.

2. If John takes his fishing pole, _____

3. If you take a tent, _____

4. If they take binoculars, _____

5. If she takes the matches, _____

6. If I _____

EXERCISE D

Read the sentences. Then join them with *but* or *if* to make one sentence. Look at the example.

1. Many people like to take vacations.
   They are expensive.

   Many people like to take vacations, but they
   are expensive.

2. Traveling is less expensive.
   People camp.

   _____

   _____

3. They don't have to pay for motels.
   They have to buy tents and sleeping bags.

   _____

   _____

4. They can sleep in a campground.
   They have sleeping bags.

   _____

   _____

5. They are more comfortable.
   They have a tent.

   _____

   _____

6. They can cook breakfast.
   They have a portable stove.

   _____

   _____

7. The Jeffersons don't have a stove.
   They can build a fire.

   _____

   _____

8. They cooked delicious pancakes.
   They forgot to bring the syrup.

   _____

   _____

9. The bear will come into the camp.
   It smells food.

   _____

   _____

10. The bear took their food.
    It didn't hurt them.

    _____

    _____

11. The fisherman will catch a lot of fish.
    He uses good bait.

    _____

    _____

12. The fisherman caught a large fish.
    It got away.

    _____

    _____

Old Faithful

EXERCISE E

Read the paragraph about Yellowstone National Park. Then fill in each space with a pronoun. Look at the example.

Yellowstone National Park is the most famous park in the United States. _It_ is in three states. _____ are Wyoming, Montana, and Idaho. There are many beautiful places to see in Yellowstone. The most famous place is Old Faithful. _____ is a geyser. _____ throws water high into the air. _____ erupts regularly every thirty-three to ninety-three minutes. Yellowstone is also famous for its lakes and rivers. Many people camp near _____ every year. _____ fish in the lakes and catch trout. _____ is the most popular fish. There are also many wild animals in Yellowstone. _____ is most famous for its bears. _____ sometimes visit the campers at night. The fishing, camping, bears, and Old Faithful have helped to make Yellowstone Park famous all over the world.

The Grand Canyon

EXERCISE F

Read the paragraph. Fill in each blank with any word that completes the meaning. Look at the example.

The Grand Canyon is one of _the_ most beautiful sights in the world. _____ is 1 mile deep _____ eighteen miles wide. It is 277 _____ long. The Colorado River helped make _____ . Millions of visitors go there _____ year. Most of the numerous visitors _____ tourists. They want to look at _____ beautiful mountains. In the summer, many _____ go camping at the Grand Canyon. _____ bring tents and sleeping bags and _____ for a few days. They can _____ many different things. They can drive _____ the top of the Canyon and _____ down to the river. They often _____ and take pictures. Some of the _____ ride bicycles along the top of _____ . Canyon. Other people walk or hike _____ the Grand Canyon. Many people like _____ hike in the Grand Canyon. Some _____ ride mules into the Canyon. Others _____ boats down the river. There are _____ things to do in this lovely _____ .

Writing Practice A. A hobby is something you do in your free time. Many campers have hobbies. They often take cameras with them. Their hobby is photography. Other hobbies are fishing, bird watching, hiking, and reading. What is your hobby?

_____

Write a few sentences about your hobby. Begin with this sentence:

   My hobby is _____ , and I enjoy it because _____ .
For example:

   My hobby is sewing and I enjoy it because it helps me relax.
   My hobby is stamp collecting and I enjoy it because I learn about different countries.

_____
_____
_____
_____
_____
_____
_____

Discuss the paragraph and possible revisions with your teacher. Then revise and rewrite it.

Writing Practice B. Look at the picture above and tell a story about it. Here are some words you can use.

grill	start the fire	watch
help	charcoal	

_____

_____

Lesson 20
REVIEW

EXERCISE A

Read the sentences. Then combine them with *and, but, so, because,* or *when.* Be careful with punctuation. Look at the example.

1. The Taylors bought a small farm in eastern Oregon.
   They went there to live last summer.

   <u>The Taylors bought a small farm in eastern Oregon,</u>
   <u>and they went there to live last summer.</u>

2. They wanted to live there.
   Not many other people live there.

   _____

   _____

3. There are no large cities.
   There are only a few small towns.

   _____

   _____

4. They needed a truck to work on the farm.
   They bought an old, used one.

   _____

   _____

5. They didn't have enough money.
   They got a loan from the bank.

   _____

   _____

6. The truck is old.
   It runs very well.

   _____

   _____

7. The road to their house is very narrow.
   It is not paved.

   _____

   _____

8. They cannot leave the farm.
   It snows.

   _____

   _____

9. They have some water.
   Mr. Taylor dug a well.

   _____

   _____

10. They get their water from the well.
    They get their water from the rain.

    _____

    _____

11. It doesn't rain in the summer.
    There is no water in the well.

    _____

    _____

12. They have to buy water.
    There is no water in the well and there is no rain.

    _____

    _____

EXERCISE B

Read these phrases, and then complete the sentences. Look at the example.

1. Exercise is important for your health because _you can_
   become strong.

2. Many people exercise before _____
   _____

3. After you exercise, _____
   _____

4. If you get tired, _____
   _____

5. Your heart is stronger when _____
   _____

6. Exercise is good for you, but _____
   _____

7. You should warm up before _____
   _____

EXERCISE C

Read the groups of words. Then use them to write complete sentences about baseball. Look at the example.

1. baseball/popular game/ U.S.

   Baseball is a popular game in the U.S.

2. boys/girls/play/school

3. high school students

4. almost every high school/team

5. almost every university/United States/team

6. many professional teams

7. professional players/earn/money

8. nine players/team

9. two teams/game

10. players/need/ball/bat/glove

11. player/hit/ball/bat

12. player/run/field

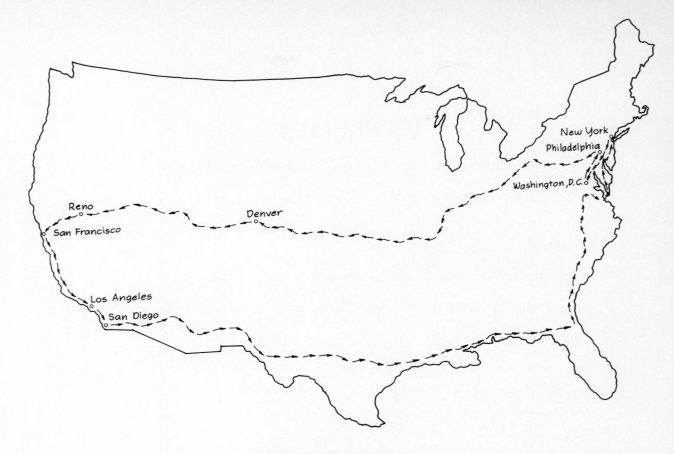

EXERCISE D

Read the paragraph and complete it. Fill in each space with the past form of a verb.

My friends and I ____took____ a trip through the United States last summer. First, we _____ a car in New York City. We _____ not _____ much money, so we _____ to camp. We _____ a tent and some sleeping bags. We _____ to cook some of our food outside, so we _____ a portable stove. We _____ everything in the car and _____ to Washington, D.C. We _____ a beautiful campground ten minutes from the capital. After we _____ the capital, we _____ to Philadelphia. We _____ Independence Hall and other historic sites. We _____ tired of camping, so we _____ in a motel one night and _____ dinner in a restaurant. We _____ west through Ohio, Illinois, Missouri, and Kansas. We _____ in Denver, Colorado, for three days because we _____ friends there. Then we _____ to California, but we _____ in Reno, Nevada. We _____ some money in Reno, but not very much. Finally, we _____ in California. We _____ San Francisco, Los Angeles, and San Diego. We _____ to New York by way of Arizona, New Mexico, Texas,

Louisiana, Alabama, Florida, and then north to New York. We _____
most nights, but we _____ in motels every four or five days. We really
_____ the United States from the ground up.

EXERCISE E

Tell about a trip you once took. Begin with this sentence:

_____ years ago, I took a _____ trip from _____ to _____ .

For example:

Three years ago, I took a wonderful trip from Tucson to Hawaii.
or
Two years ago, I took a terrible camping trip in the mountains.

_____

_____

_____

_____

_____

_____

_____

_____

_____

_____

Discuss the paragraph and possible revisions with your teacher. Then revise and
rewrite it.

Unit III
Lesson 21

PARAGRAPHS THAT GIVE INSTRUCTIONS

Objectives in order of importance:

 paragraph organization

 main-idea sentence

 controlling idea

 transitions

 revising work

 organize work before writing

In Lesson 21, you are going to write two paragraphs that tell how to do something. These paragraphs will give instructions. Look at the following example:

HOW TO GET A DRIVER'S LICENSE

It is easy to get a driver's license if you follow these steps. First, get a driver's manual and study it carefully. Second, go to the Department of Motor Vehicles in your city. Fill out an application, show your old license, and pay the application fee. Third, take the written test. Then an officer will give you an eye test. Finally, another officer will take your picture. You will receive your license in the mail in six to eight weeks.

People usually write paragraphs about a single topic. Several sentences about one idea or topic make *a paragraph*. Each paragraph has one *main idea*. A paragraph usually begins with *a main-idea sentence*. This sentence tells about the paragraph, and it is an introduction for the reader. All the information in the paragraph is about the same main idea.

When you write a paragraph, you must do four things. First, you must *indent* the first line. Indent means to leave a space at the beginning of the paragraph. It tells the reader that a new topic is beginning. Second, write the sentences of the paragraph one after another. Third, begin each sentence with a *capital letter*. Last, put a *period* at the end of each sentence.

EXERCISE A

This paragraph explains how to get a driver's license. There are six steps. Reread the paragraph and list the six steps below.

1. _____
2. _____
3. _____
4. _____
5. _____
6. _____

CHRONOLOGICAL ORDER

Chronological order means in order of time. Certain words in English show time sequence. Some of these words are listed below.

first	then
second	after that
third	next
fourth	last
	finally

EXERCISE B

Reread ''How to Get a Driver's License.'' Circle the sequence words. Notice how they join the six steps in Exercise A.

PUNCTUATION

Use a comma after the sequence words listed earlier. For example:

Third, take the written test.

Before and *after* also show time sequence.
Use a comma in the middle of the sentence when the sentence begins with *before,* *after*, or *if.*

Before you go to the Department of Motor Vehicles, study the book.
After you fill out the application, take the written test.

Paragraph 1: How to Buy a Car

PART I

With your teacher and classmates, write down a list of five things that you need to do in order to buy a car.

1. _____
2. _____
3. _____
4. _____
5. _____

PART II

1. Look at the steps you listed. Be sure that they are in the correct chronological order. You may want to change some sentences or the order of some sentences.

2. Are the sentences in Exercise A a paragraph? Why not? They are not a paragraph because they do not contain a main-idea sentence or sequence words.

3. Before you write your paragraph "How to Buy a Car," write the sequence words you will use to join the steps in the paragraph. Write the sequence words in the left margin of Part I.

PART III

1. Discuss the organization of your paragraph with your teacher.
2. Ask your teacher to correct the sentences in Part I.

PART IV

1. You are ready to write your paragraph. Use the steps and sequence words you listed in Part I. Remember to indent your paragraph and write each sentence after the other.
2. Use this main-idea sentence: "It is not difficult to buy a car if you are careful and do these things."

HOW TO BUY A CAR

_____

_____

_____

_____

_____

_____

_____

_____

_____

_____

_____

_____

EXERCISE C

Punctuation. Read the paragraph. Then punctuate it, using commas and capital letters.

HOW TO OPEN A SAVINGS ACCOUNT

it is easy to open a savings account at a bank if you follow these steps. first go to the new-accounts clerk and say that you want to open a savings account. second fill out an application form. before you give the clerk your money sign some papers. finally the clerk will give you a savings book.

Dictation. With your classmates and teacher, write a very short paragraph explaining how to open a checking account. Use sequence words and a main-idea sentence.

HOW TO OPEN A CHECKING ACCOUNT

_____

_____

_____

_____

EXERCISE D

Read the paragraph. Fill in each space with a sequence word.

HOW TO USE A PAY TELEPHONE

It is easy to use a pay telephone is you follow these steps. _____ , pick up the receiver. _____ , put a quarter, twenty-five cents, in the slot. Wait for the dial tone. _____ you hear the dial tone, dial the number. _____ wait for your friend to answer the phone. _____ , don't talk too long!

EXERCISE E

Read these sentences. They will make a paragraph. Decide on their correct order and write the numbers in the margin. Then copy the sentences in the form of a paragraph. Remember to indent.

____ Cook the rice for about twenty minutes.

____ First, wash the rice carefully.

____ When the oil is hot, brown one cup of rice for a few minutes.

____ When the water boils, turn down the heat to simmer.

____ Finally, serve it with meat and vegetables.

_1_ If you follow these steps, it is not difficult to make rice.

____ Second, heat some oil in a pot.

____ Add salt, pepper, and saffron to the oil and rice.

_6_ After you add the spices, add two cups of water.

HOW TO COOK RICE

_____

_____

_____

_____

_____

_____

_____

_____

_____

Paragraph 2: How to Make Fresh Orange Juice

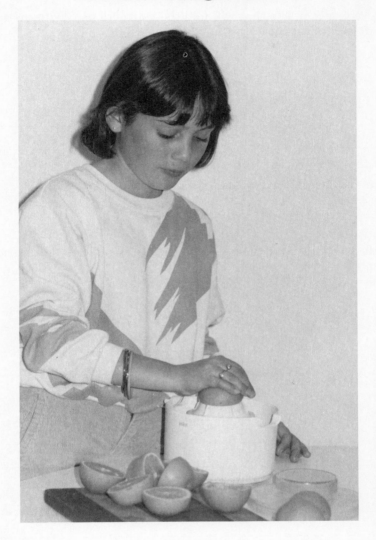

PART I

Tell how to make fresh orange juice. First make a list of instructions. Here are some words that you may need.

slice   squeeze   squeezer   pour   serve

1. _____

2. _____

3. _____

4. _____

5. _____

PART II

1. Check your instructions. Are they in the correct order?
2. List the sequence words that will join the instructions. Write the sequence words in the left margin of Part I.

PART III

1. Write a main-idea sentence.

_____

_____

2. Discuss the organization with your teacher.
3. Ask your teacher to correct the sentences in Part I.

PART IV

You are ready to write your paragraph. Use the main-idea sentence from Part III and the list and sequence words from Part I.

**HOW TO MAKE
FRESH ORANGE JUICE**

_____

_____

_____

_____

_____

_____

_____

_____

_____

_____

_____

_____

_____

_____

_____

_____

Lesson 22
PARAGRAPHS THAT DESCRIBE

In Lesson 22 you are going to write two paragraphs that describe a room and an animal. To *describe* means to make a picture with words. Read this example about a pleasant room in a child's house, and try to see it in your mind.

A MOST PLEASANT ROOM

The most pleasant room in my house is the library. We call it the library because we keep all our books there. Two walls of the room have book shelves. My mother's large desk is under the shelves against one wall. We have a small desk beside mother's large one. There is a tall bookcase against the third wall next to a closet. There is also a small bookcase for my sister and me. We keep our books and games there. There is a long work table under the window on the other wall. The computer and sewing machine are on this table. In the middle of the room, there is open space. There is a carpet on the floor. We often sit on it to read or play games. The whole family spends many hours in this room together. It is a library, work room, and family room.

What is the main-idea sentence? _____

_____

In what part of the room does the description start?

_____

A descriptive paragraph usually begins in one place. Then it moves around in an orderly way. Notice that in this example, the description begins with two walls. Then it describes the third wall, fourth wall, and the center of the room. In order to show where things are, the writer uses prepositions of place to direct the reader. Reread the descriptive paragraph and circle the prepositions of place.

PREPOSITIONS OF PLACE

in the middle of	next to	in
in front of	beside	on
in back of	near	by
	over	at
	under	of
	between	

EXERCISE A

Read the following paragraph and fill in each space with a preposition. Look at the example.

THE DOCTOR'S OFFICE

I feel sick and I am tired, but the doctor's office seems cheerful to me. The room is long and narrow. The door is __*at*__ one end. _____ the other end _____ the room, there is a large window. Outside the window, there is a small garden. There are two tall palm trees and several cacti _____ the garden. There is a long low table _____ the window. There is a large leafy green plant _____ the table. _____ the corner, next to the table, there is a small palm tree _____ a pot. _____ the two side walls, there are rows of large, comfortable chairs. There are several big, colorful pictures _____ the walls _____ back _____ the chairs. There are also two rows of chairs _____ the middle of the room. There are some tables _____ the chairs. Many magazines are _____ the tables. The room is an attractive place to wait for the doctor.

Reread the paragraph, and draw a picture of the doctor's office.

EXERCISE B

Look at the picture above. Then write a few sentences about it, telling where the things are. Use prepositions.

_____

_____

_____

_____

_____

PUNCTUATION

Put a comma after a prepositional phrase at the beginning of the sentence.

Under the window, there is a long worktable.
In the middle of the room, there is open space.

EXERCISE C

Read the paragraph and punctuate it. Add capital letters, commas, and periods.

OUR KITCHEN

our kitchen is very modern and convenient it has many appliances to make cooking easy and fast there is a large self-cleaning stove with a microwave oven. near the stove there is an electric mixer a blender and a food processor. on the counter to the right of the stove there is a toaster an electric can-opener a coffee grinder and a coffeepot. the refrigerator is in the corner of the kitchen it has an automatic ice maker and it is self-defrosting. the automatic dishwasher is next to the sink. everything in the kitchen is electric and automatic. cooking dinner doesn't take any time at all

Paragraph 1: Your Classroom

You are going to describe your classroom, but first, look around it. Think of one word to describe the room. Is it beautiful? pleasant? attractive? dark? empty? cold? unpleasant? bright? crowded?

This word will be the controlling idea in your paragraph. It should be in the main-idea sentence.

Write a main-idea sentence for your paragraph about your classroom.

_____

_____

Why is your room this way? Make a list of all the things in the room that make it _____ .

1. _____
2. _____
3. _____
4. _____
5. _____
6. _____

Arrange your list in spatial order. Use prepositions of place to show where things are in the room.

Ask your teacher to check your sentences and organization. When you have revised your sentences, write the paragraph. Begin with the main-idea sentence and controlling idea. Move around the room in order and use prepositions of place.

OUR CLASSROOM

_____
_____
_____
_____
_____
_____
_____
_____
_____
_____

Throughout history, there have been many imaginary animals. They did not live, but people believed in them. They described them, and other people were able to "see" them. Read about the unicorn, an imaginary animal (Figure 22-1).

THE UNICORN

The unicorn was a beautiful and gentle animal. It looked like a horse. It had a white body, and a purple head, with blue eyes. In the center of its forehead, there was a long horn with a red tip. The horn was very strong. Unicorns were able to run so fast that it was very difficult to catch one. They were strong animals, but they were very gentle with young girls. A young girl was able to touch the unicorn with her hand. The unicorn might even sleep with its head in her lap.

Read the paragraph. What are the two controlling ideas?

_____ and _____

List all the words that show the unicorn was beautiful.

_____

Tell why the unicorn was gentle.

_____

FIGURE 22-1

DESCRIPTIONS

When you describe something, it is sometimes useful to compare it to something else.

The unicorn looked like a horse.

The unicorn was like a horse.

The unicorn was similar to a horse.

EXERCISE D

Read this paragraph. Fill in each space with a verb. Use the past.

DRAGONS

Dragons _were_ also imaginary animals. Most dragons _____ like snakes or lizards. They _____ scales on their long, thin bodies. They _____ four legs with large, long claws. The head and front legs sometimes _____ like a crocodile's or a lizard's. Many dragons _____ wings, and they _____ able to fly. In Europe, people thought that dragons _____ bad. Dragons sometimes breathed fire, and smoke _____ out of their noses.

EXERCISE E

Read this description and try to guess what animal it is.

WHAT IS ITS NAME?

This animal is very useful to people. It has a very long curved neck. At the end of its long neck is a small head with small ears and a long, flat nose. It has four very long legs with large, round, flat feet. In spite of its long legs, the animal walks gracefully and proudly, and it can run very quickly. People sometimes use it for races. More often, however, people use it for transportation in the desert because it can live for a long time without water. Also, it can walk easily on the desert because of its large flat feet. There are two kinds of this animal. One kind has one large hump on its back and lives on the Arabian peninsula. The other kind has two large humps on its back and lives in Asia.

What animal is this?_____

What is the controlling idea?_____

How do people use this animal?

1. _____

2. _____

Paragraph 2: Describe an Animal

You are going to describe an animal. It may be imaginary or real. Plan your paragraph before you begin to write.

First, write down the name of an animal. _____

What is your controlling idea? _____

Write the main-idea sentence, and include the controlling idea.

_____

_____

What is its outstanding feature?_____

What other features does it have?

_____

_____

_____

Arrange the features in order. Put the most important feature last.
When you have written your sentences and organized them, write paragraph 2.
Give it a title, and remember to indent.

_____

_____

_____

_____

_____

Lesson 23
CHRONOLOGICAL PARAGRAPHS

In Lesson 23 you are going to write two chronological paragraphs. *Chronological paragraphs* tell about people or events in order of time. They sometimes discuss something in the past. They often describe historical events or the lives of famous people.

HISTORY OF THE COMPUTER

Computers are the "new" machines of the 1980s, but someone first thought of them more than one hundred and fifty years ago. Charles Babbage designed the first computerlike machine in England in 1830. He did not finish his work, but today's computers come from his ideas. A half century later, in 1888, Herman Hollerith used a machine to help count the people in the United States. Forty years after that, an American named Vannevar Bush made the first analog computer. It helped aim guns in World War II from 1940 to 1945. Professor Howard Aiken and some engineers from IBM finished the first digital computer in 1944. Then two engineers at the University of Pennsylvania made the UNIVAC I computer, in 1951. There were many UNIVAC computers. This kind of computer was the first to be produced in large numbers.

EXERCISE A

Reread the preceding paragraph. Write down the events in the history of the computer.

1. _____

2. _____

3. _____

4. _____

5. _____

EXPRESSIONS OF TIME

Sequence words and *dates* often show chronological order. Other expressions of time also show time sequence. Look at these examples.

a half century later

more than one hundred fifty years ago

forty years after that

These words count time.

60 seconds = 1 minute	7 days = 1 week
60 minutes = 1 hour	4 weeks = 1 month
24 hours = 1 day	12 months = 1 year

10 years = 1 decade

10 decades = 1 century

100 years = 1 century

EXERCISE B

Reread "History of the Computer." Underline the expressions of time, dates, and sequence words that show the order of events in the history of computers.

EXERCISE C

Underline the main-idea sentence. It is the first sentence of the paragraph. It tells what the paragraph is about and how much time the discussion covers.

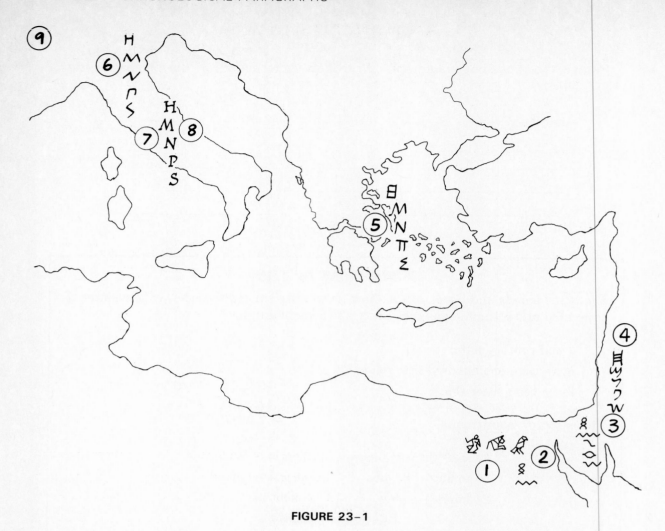

FIGURE 23-1

EXERCISE D

Read these sentences about the history of the alphabet. They are not in order. Look at the map in Figure 23-1 and put them in the correct order, writing the numbers in the margin. Then write the sentences in the form of a paragraph. Notice the main-idea sentence. Remember to indent.

____ The Egyptians wrote with pictures before 3000 B.C.

____ Several hundred years later, the Greeks learned the alphabet from the Phoenicians.

____ The alphabet began 5,000 years ago in Egypt, and has a long history.

____ By 700 B.C., the Romans had learned the alphabet from the Etruscans.

____ By 1500 B.C., Semitic writing in Syria and Palestine used pictures and letters.

____ In 800 B.C., the Etruscans in Italy wrote the Greek alphabet.

____ By 300 B.C., the Roman alphabet had twenty-three letters.

____ The Phoenicians made the first alphabet of twenty-two letters for twenty-two consonant sounds in about 1000 B.C.

____ Finally, the twenty-six-letter English alphabet came from the Roman alphabet.

HISTORY OF THE ALPHABET

_____
_____
_____
_____
_____
_____
_____
_____
_____
_____
_____
_____
_____
_____
_____
_____
_____
_____
_____
_____
_____

Many chronological paragraphs tell about the past. Write the past-tense forms of these common irregular verbs.

be	_____	begin	_____	write	_____
marry	_____	stop	_____	make	_____
take	_____	study	_____	do	_____
come	_____	teach	_____	go	_____
grow	_____	think	_____	have	_____
become	_____	be born	_____	shoot	_____

EXERCISE E

Read this paragraph about the life of Abraham Lincoln. Write the past tense of the verb in parentheses. Pay attention to the main-idea sentences and the expressions of time.

ABRAHAM LINCOLN

Abraham Lincoln _____ the sixteenth president of the United States, from
                   (be)

1861 to 1865. He _____ born on February 12, 1809, in Kentucky. He _____
          (be)   (grow)

up on farms in Kentucky and Indiana. His mother _____ when he _____
                                    (die)   (be)

nine years old. He _____ hard and _____ to school very much, but he
              (work)   (not go)

_____ to read. In 1830, his family _____ to Illinois. He _____ at many
(learn)   (move)   (work)

jobs and _____ himself law. He _____ a lawyer in 1836. Six years later,
       (teach)   (become)

he _____ Mary Todd, and they _____ four sons. In 1861, he _____
   (marry)   (have)   (become)

President of the United States. He _____ president during the Civil War.
                     (be)

Lincoln _____ that all people should be free. Eleven days after the Civil War
     (think)

_____, John Wilkes Booth _____ President Lincoln on April 14, 1865, in
(end)   (shoot)

Washington, D.C.

> **Punctuation.**   When the *time expression* is at the beginning of the sentence, use a comma after it.
>
> Six years later, Lincoln married Mary Todd.

EXERCISE F

Punctuate this paragraph about the life of Martin Luther King, Jr. Use capital letters and commas.

MARTIN LUTHER KING, JR.

martin luther king jr was a leader of the black people in the united states in the 1960s. he was born in atlanta georgia on january 15 1929. he grew up in atlanta and went to school there. he was a very good student and he finished high school when he was fifteen years old. he went to college and a university in the north. in 1953 he married corretta scott and they had four children. in 1955 he received his Ph.D. degree and the next year he became the minister of a church in montgomery alabama. he helped black people in montgomery win equal rights. martin luther king thought that people should not use violence. james earl ray killed dr. king on april 4 1968 in memphis tennessee.

Dictation. With your teacher and classmates, choose a person you all know. Write a very short paragraph about the life of this person. Choose a good main-idea sentence. Your teacher will dictate something similar.

_____

_____

_____

_____

_____

_____

_____

Paragraph 1: Biography of a Famous Person

Write a paragraph about a famous person from your country.

Name _____

PART I

Write a main-idea sentence. Include the name of the person, the name of the country, the time, and who the person was.

_____

_____

PART II

Write down the important events in this person's life. Start with birth.

1. _____

2. _____

3. _____

4. _____

5. _____

Find the dates of these events. Decide which expressions of time you will use. Write the time expression or date for each event in the left margin.

PART III

Discuss the organization of your paragraph with your teacher and ask him or her to check your sentences.

PART IV

When you have revised your sentences, write the paragraph. Copy your main-idea sentence, and be sure that the events are in chronological order. Use time expressions and dates. Give your paragraph a title, and remember to indent.

_____

_____

_____

_____

_____

_____

_____

_____

_____

_____

_____

EXERCISE G

Read the following paragraph about space shuttles. Fill in each blank with a pronoun. Look at the example.

SPACE SHUTTLES

In April 1981, the Columbia Space Shuttle was the first spacecraft to go into space and to return to earth. Since then, __*it*__ has made many trips into orbit around the earth. There were only two astronauts on the first flight. _____ were John W. Young and Robert L. Crippen. _____ did many things in space and orbited the earth many times before _____ returned to earth on April 14. The spacecraft landed like an airplane, in the Mojave Desert in California.

In October 1984, *Challenger* made the thirteenth space-shuttle flight. _____ carried five men and two women astronauts into space. The commander was Robert L. Crippen. _____ was making his fourth trip into space. Marc Garneau was the first Canadian to go into space. _____ is a physicist. Sally Ride was also a passenger. _____ was the first American woman to go into space, in 1983. _____ was making her second trip. Another woman was on the flight. _____ was the first American woman to walk in space. The flight was 3.5 million miles long and _____ lasted eight days. While _____ were in space, the astronauts studied the Earth and took pictures of _____. This flight was the first of regular monthly shuttle flights. Now the space shuttle will return to space monthly, and _____ will carry astronauts, passengers, and cargo.

Paragraph 2: An Important Event

Write a paragraph about an important event either in your life or in the history of your country.

Event _____

PART I

Write a main-idea sentence. Be sure to include the event, the date, the place, and the people.

_____

_____

PART II

Make a list of things that happened.

1. _____
2. _____
3. _____
4. _____
5. _____
6. _____

Find out the dates. Choose the time expressions. Write the dates, time expressions, or sequence words in the margin.

PART III

After you revise your sentences in Part II, write the paragraph.

_____

_____

_____

_____

_____

_____

_____

Lesson 24
PARAGRAPHS THAT COMPARE AND CONTRAST

Paragraphs that Compare

In Lesson 24 you are going to write three paragraphs that compare and contrast. Paragraphs that compare show similarity. They tell in what ways two things are the same. Read the paragraph about the camel and the llama. It tells about five similarities. List them.

1. _____
2. _____
3. _____
4. _____
5. _____

The Camel and the Llama

The camel and the llama come from different parts of the world, but they are similar animals. First, both animals belong to the Camelidae family, and they are similar in ap-

180

pearance. Both animals have long necks, small heads, and very long, thin legs with two toes. In addition, both animals are domesticated. They are not wild animals; they work for people. People use the camel and llama as pack animals. The llama can carry up to 60 kilos (130 pounds). People also use these two animals for clothes and food. They use the wool, the hide, the milk, and the meat. Another similarity between the two animals is their temperament. Both are usually calm and quiet, but when they are tired or angry, they kick and spit. The most important similarity is that they are both well adapted to their environment. The llama can breathe and work at high mountain altitudes, and the camel can live and work in the hot, dry deserts. The camel and the llama are not only similar in appearance, but they are very useful to people.

Underline the first sentence of the paragraph. It is the main-idea sentence. In paragraphs that compare, the main-idea sentence must answer two questions.

1. What two things does the paragraph talk about?
2. Are they similar?

Certain transition words help list the similarities. They are *both, also, too, another, in addition,* and *furthermore.* Reread the paragraph and underline the transition words.

PUNCTUATION

Use a comma after introductory phrases such as *in addition* and *furthermore.*

In addition, both animals are domesticated.
Furthermore, their personalities are similar.

EXERCISE A

Read the paragraph about Ping-Pong and tennis. Fill in the spaces with appropriate transitions.

PING-PONG AND TENNIS

Ping-Pong and tennis are two sports that use very different-sized courts, but the games are very similar. _____ , the equipment is similar. A net divides each court into two halves. The players hit a ball over the net with a paddle or racket. _____ _____ is the scoring. Players score a point when the opponent does not return the ball. Both sports have games and matches. Players must win a game by at least two points. To win the match, a player must win two out of three or three out of five games. _____ , the same number of players can play either Ping-Pong or tennis. There are games for singles and doubles. In singles, there is only one player on each team. In doubles, there are two players on each team. The court for both Ping-Pong and tennis is larger for doubles play. The _____ similarity is the play. In both sports, one player serves the ball and the opponent must return it. The players volley until one player misses the ball. The equipment, the scoring, the players, and the play in Ping-Pong and tennis are so similar that they are almost the same game.

EXERCISE B

Read the paragraph about bicyclists and drivers. It is not a good paragraph. Make it better. Add a main-idea sentence, combine sentences, and add transition words. Be careful of punctuation.

   Bicycles and cars are different vehicles. Bicyclists must obey traffic laws. Drivers must obey the same traffic laws. Bicyclists and drivers must stop at red lights and stop signs. Bicyclists and drivers must give signals before they turn. Bicyclists and drivers must watch out for pedestrians. They must stop for pedestrians in a crosswalk. Bicyclists must watch out for drivers. Drivers must watch out for bicyclists. Bicyclists and drivers sometimes have the same problems. Bicyclists sometimes have flat tires. Drivers sometimes have flat tires. When they have flat tires, they must stop and change them. Cars are faster than bicycles. Bicycles and cars are two kinds of transportation.

Paragraph 1: Fast Food Restaurants

EXERCISE C

Compare two fast-food restaurants. Tell how they are the same. Choose two that you know, such as a MacDonalds, Burger King, Jack in the Box, Taco Bell, Church's Fried Chicken, or any other. Write a main-idea sentence. Use transition words. You might compare these things:

menu

fast service

interior of restaurant

location

price

drive-through

_____

_____

_____

_____

_____

_____

Paragraphs that Contrast

Paragraphs that contrast, show differences. Read the paragraph about soccer and football. It tells about five differences. List them.

1. _____
2. _____
3. _____
4. _____
5. _____

SOCCER OR FOOTBALL?

People sometimes call soccer "football"; however, soccer and football are two very different games. First, the fields are different sizes. A soccer field is larger than a football field. It is 110 meters (120 yards) long and 70 meters (75 yards) wide. The football field, however, is 100 yards (91 meters) long and 160 feet (49 meters) wide. Another difference is game length. A soccer match is ninety minutes long, and is divided into two halves. On the other hand, a football game is sixty minutes long. It is divided into four quarters. A third difference is the score. When a soccer player kicks the ball through the goal, that is called a goal, and all goals score one point. In contrast, when a football player carries the ball between the goal posts, it is called a touchdown. A touchdown is worth six points. Another difference is the ball. A soccer ball is round, while the football is oval. The biggest difference in the two games is the play. In soccer, the players cannot touch the ball with their hands or arms. The players cannot touch the players on the other team, either. In football, however, the players can carry the ball in their arms, throw it, or kick it to another player. Players may also tackle players on the other team. To tackle means to pull the other player down, so that he falls and drops the ball. Soccer and football are very different games. Almost everything—including the field, the length of the game, the scoring, the ball, and the play—are very different.

Look at the first sentence. Underline it. It is the main-idea sentence. It answers two important questions.

1. What two things does the paragraph discuss?
2. Does the paragraph talk about the differences?

Look at this outline for the paragraph.

1. the field
   a. soccer
   b. football
2. the length of the game
   a. soccer
   b. football
3. the scoring
   a. soccer
   b. football

    4. the ball
      a. soccer
      b. football
    5. the play
      a. soccer
      b. football

For each difference listed, soccer is discussed first. The order—soccer, football—is important. It should not change in the middle of the paragraph. When you write, pay attention to order.

Some common transition words that show contrast are *but, however, in contrast*, and *on the other hand*. Underline the transitions that show contrast in the paragraph about soccer and football.

PUNCTUATION

Use a comma after a phrase at the beginning of a sentence.

> On the other hand, the football is oval.
> On the contrary, the football field is much smaller.
> However, football players can carry and throw the ball.

However may be used in the middle of the sentence. In that case, use two commas: one before and one after.

> Football players, however, can carry and throw the ball.

EXERCISE D

Read the paragraph about calendars. Fill in the blanks with transition words or phrases that show contrast.

CALENDARS

    Both the Muslim calendar and the Gregorian calendar measure time, but they are quite different because one is lunar and the other is solar. The Muslim calendar is a lunar calendar. It divides the year into months by the moon. Each new month starts with a new moon. _____ , the Gregorian calendar divides the year into months by the sun. The number of days in the year is also different in the two calendars. There are 354 days in the Muslim calendar, and sometimes there are 355 days. There are twelve months in the lunar calendar, and each month has 29 or 30 days.

_____ , there are 365 days in the Gregorian calendar, and sometimes there are 366. There are twelve months, but they are 30 or 31 days long. _____ , the biggest difference between the Muslim and Gregorian calendars is the date of the seasons. Because the Muslim calendar uses the moon, the dates of the seasons change every year. For example, spring will begin on a different date each year. In the Gregorian calendar, _____ , the seasons are on the same date each year. The first day of spring is always on the same date. Many people in the world use each calendar to measure time, but because one uses the moon and the other uses the sun, they are quite different.

EXERCISE E

The sentences in this paragraph are very short. Combine them to make the paragraph more interesting. Add transitions.

BRONTOSAURUS
AND
TYRANNOSAURUS

Brontosaurus was a very large dinosaur. Tyrannosaurus was a very large dinosaur. They had different diets. They had different temperaments. Brontosaurus ate plants. It had a long neck. It had a very long tail. It was able to eat leaves on tall trees. Tyrannosaurus ate meat. It had very sharp teeth. It had very sharp claws. It sometimes ate other plant-eating dinosaurs. Brontosaurus walked on all four legs. Tyrannosaurus walked only on its two back legs. Brontosaurus was a peaceful dinosaur. It was very calm and gentle. Tyrannosaurus was a very fierce dinosaur. It was terrible. Although they were both very large dinosaurs, Brontosaurus and Tyrannosaurus were very different in appearance, diet, and temperament.

Paragraph 2: My Hometown

Write a paragraph about your hometown. Contrast your hometown as it is now and as it was a hundred years ago. Before you begin, choose four areas that you want to talk about. Some things you might contrast are size, population, transportation, shopping, entertainment, economics, racial mix, medical facilities, or educational facilities.

1. _____

2. _____

3. _____

4. _____

Decide whether you want to talk about now or a hundred years ago first. Be sure to use the same order for each of the four items.

Write a main-idea sentence. Be sure that you include the name of your town, the two time periods, and that it has changed.

_____

_____

_____

Now you are ready to write your paragraph.

_____

_____

_____

_____

_____

_____

_____

_____

_____

_____

_____

Paragraph 3

Write a comparison/contrast paragraph about two things. You may choose two people, two rooms, two animals, or two towns. Make a plan before you start. Pay attention to the main-idea sentence and transition words. After your teacher corrects the first draft, revise and rewrite it.

_____

_____

_____

_____

_____

_____

_____

_____

_____

_____

_____

_____

Appendix A
COMMON IRREGULAR VERBS

Simple form	ing form	Past
be (am, is, are)	being	was, were
become	becoming	became
begin	beginning	began
bring	bringing	brought
buy	buying	bought
choose	choosing	chose
come	coming	came
die	dying	died
do	doing	did
drink	drinking	drank
drive	driving	drove
eat	eating	ate
fall	falling	fell
feed	feeding	fed
fly	flying	flew
feel	feeling	felt
find	finding	found
forget	forgetting	forgot
get	getting	got
give	giving	gave
go	going	went
grow	growing	grew
have	having	had
hear	hearing	heard
hold	holding	held
hurt	hurting	hurt

know	knowing	knew
lead	leading	led
leave	leaving	left
lend	lending	lent
let	letting	let
lose	losing	lost
make	making	made
meet	meeting	met
pay	paying	paid
put	putting	put
quit	quitting	quit
read	reading	read
ride	riding	rode
run	running	ran
say	saying	said
see	seeing	saw
sell	selling	sold
shoot	shooting	shot
shut	shutting	shut
sing	singing	sang
sit	sitting	sat
sleep	sleeping	slept
speak	speaking	spoke
spend	spending	spent
swim	swimming	swam
take	taking	took
teach	teaching	taught
tell	telling	told
think	thinking	thought
throw	throwing	threw
understand	understanding	understood
wear	wearing	wore
win	winning	won
write	writing	wrote

Appendix B

PUNCTUATION RULES

Period

1. at the end of a sentence
2. for an abbreviation
   Jan.
3. after a title
   Dr. King

Question mark

1. at the end of a question
   Did you see the book?

Apostrophe

1. in contractions
   I'm   What's
2. to show possession
   Linda's father (singular)
   the girls' brother (plural)

Capital letters

1. the pronoun I
2. at the beginning of a sentence
3. names:
people	Mahatma Gandhi
countries	Saudi Arabia
cities	Rabat
states	California
universities	New York University
mountains	Mt. Everest
rivers	the Mississippi River
lakes	the Great Lakes

deserts	the Sahara Desert
seas	the Mediterranean Sea
oceans	the Pacific Ocean
languages	English
nationality	the French girl
days of the week	Wednesday
months of the year	February
holidays	Thanksgiving
religions	Islam
titles	Mrs. Bonsall
degrees	Ph.D.
*directions	the East, the South

Commas

1. in numbers to separate thousands
   1,000,000

2. between words in a series
   September, April, June, and November

3. between the day and year in dates
   Monday, August 5, 1945, is my birthdate.

4. between the city and country
   Bogota, Colombia

5. after clauses at the beginning of the sentence
   When I came to the U.S., I studied English.
   If I have time tonight, I will visit you.
   Because the weather was bad, we didn't go camping.

6. phrases of time and location at the beginning of the sentence
   In the corner, there is a large palm tree.
   More than a century ago, there was no electricity.

7. before and, but, and so when they join two main clauses.
   My friend went shopping, but he forgot the milk.

8. after yes or no at the beginning of the sentence
   Yes, I'll be glad to.

---

*Capitalize *directions* only when they refer to a specific section of the country

Appendix C
SPELLING RULES

Words that End in
s, z, x, sh, or *ch*

If a noun or a verb ends in a *s, z, x, sh,* or *ch,* add *es* to form the third person singular verb and the plural noun.

box	boxes	quiz	quizzes	church	churches
bush	bushes	grass	grasses	lunch	lunches

Words that End in a *y*

If a word ends in a *y* preceded by a consonant, change the *y* to *i* and add *ed* or *es* to verbs and nouns or *er* or *est* to adjectives.

study	studies	studied	lady	ladies
try	tries	tried	city	cities
pretty	prettier	prettiest		
ugly	uglier	ugliest		

Words that End with an *e*

If a one syllable verb or an adjective ends in an *e*, drop the *e* before adding *er, est, ing,* or *ed*.

large	larger	largest
late	later	latest
examine	examining	examined
practice	practicing	practiced

Words that End
in a Single Consonant

If a verb or adjective ends in a single consonant preceded by a single vowel, double the final consonant before adding *er, est, ing,* or *ed.*

big	bigger	biggest
red	redder	reddest
run	running	
swim	swimming	

Nouns that End in *f*

With some nouns, final *f* changes to *v* before adding *s* or *es.*

knife	knives	wife	wives	shelf	shelves
half	halves	loaf	loaves	life	lives
leaf	leaves				